Math Engagement:
Grade 5

By
M.J. OWEN

COPYRIGHT © 2003 Mark Twain Media, Inc.

ISBN 1-58037-233-3

Printing No. CD-1579

Mark Twain Media, Inc., Publishers
Distributed by Carson-Dellosa Publishing Company, Inc.

The purchase of this book entitles the buyer to reproduce the student pages for classroom use only. Other permissions may be obtained by writing Mark Twain Media, Inc., Publishers.

Standards reprinted with permission from *Principles and Standards for School Mathematics,* copyright 2000 by the National Council of Teachers of Mathematics. All rights reserved. No endorsement by NCTM is implied.

All rights reserved. Printed in the United States of America.

Table of Contents

Introduction

Based on the National Council of Teachers of Mathematics (NCTM) Standards, this series provides students with multiple grade-appropriate opportunities to practice each skill. Each book contains several practice pages targeting each skill, as well as an assessment page at the end of each section. The book also includes periodic reviews of multiple skills throughout the book, in addition to a cumulative assessment. Each assessment and review is set up in standardized-test format.

Page no.	Number and Operations	Algebra	Geometry	Measurement	Data Analysis, Probability	Problem Solving	Reasoning, Proof	Communication	Connections	Representation
2	x							x		
3	x							x		
4	x									
5	x									
6	x									
7	x					x				
8	x									
9	x								x	
10	x				x					
11	x					x				
12	x									
13	x								x	
14	x									
15	x									
16	x									
17	x					x				
18	x					x				
19	x									
20	x									
21	x						x			
22	x					x				
23		x							x	
24		x								
25		x				x			x	
26		x								
27		x							x	
28		x				x				
29		x								
30		x								
31			x							x
32			x			x				
33			x			x				
34			x			x				
35			x			x				
36			x							
37			x							
38			x							
39			x						x	
40			x							
41			x	x						
42			x							
43			x			x				

Page no.	Number and Operations	Algebra	Geometry	Measurement	Data Analysis, Probability	Problem Solving	Reasoning, Proof	Communication	Connections	Representation
44		x				x				
45		x								
46		x		x						
47		x								
48		x								
49		x		x						
50		x								
51		x		x	x					
52		x				x	x		x	x
53		x				x				x
54			x							
55			x							
56			x					x		
57			x					x		
58			x							
59			x							
60			x							x
61			x							
62			x					x	x	
63			x							
64			x							
65			x	x						
66			x							
67				x	x			x		
68				x	x			x		
69				x	x			x		
70				x	x					
71				x	x			x		x
72				x	x				x	
73				x	x				x	
74				x	x	x				
75				x					x	
76				x						
77				x						
78				x	x	x	x			
79				x						
80				x						
81				x	x			x		
82				x	x					
83				x	x	x				
86	x	x	x	x	x					

Name: _____ Date: _____

Skill: Understanding numbers, ways of representing numbers, relationships among numbers, and number systems

Unit 1: Number and Operations: *Practice Activity 1*

Did you know that there are many ways to write the same number? Try writing each of the following numbers in three different forms: word form, standard form, and expanded form. Look at the examples before you get started.

Example: 5,987,978
word form: five million, nine hundred eighty-seven thousand, nine hundred
        seventy-eight
standard form: 5,987,978
expanded form: 5,000,000 + 900,000 + 80,000 + 7,000 + 900 + 70 + 8

Example: 32.547
word form: thirty-two and five hundred forty-seven thousandths
standard form: 32.547
expanded form: 30 + 2 + 0.5 + 0.04 + 0.007

---

1. 898,432

   word form: _____

   standard form: _____

   expanded form: _____

2. 5,001

   word form: _____

   standard form: _____

   expanded form: _____

3. 3,212,098

   word form: _____

   standard form: _____

   expanded form: _____

4. 14,342,009

   word form: _____

   standard form: _____

   expanded form: _____

5. 23,098

   word form: _____

   standard form: _____

   expanded form: _____

Name: _____ Date: _____

Unit 1: Number and Operations: *Practice Activity 1 (cont.)*

6. 789,543

word form: _____

standard form: _____

expanded form: _____

7. 9,001,987

word form: _____

standard form: _____

expanded form: _____

8. 12,987

word form: _____

standard form: _____

expanded form: _____

9. 21,234,231

word form: _____

standard form: _____

expanded form: _____

10. 543,323

word form: _____

standard form: _____

expanded form: _____

11. 70.08

word form: _____

standard form: _____

expanded form: _____

12. 6.55

word form: _____

standard form: _____

expanded form: _____

13. 0.065

word form: _____

standard form: _____

expanded form: _____

© Mark Twain Media, Inc., Publishers

Name: _____ Date: _____

Skill: Understanding numbers, ways of representing numbers, relationships among numbers, and number systems

Unit 1: Number and Operations: *Practice Activity 2*

Just a Tip: The value of a number depends on the place that it holds. Try making a place value chart for each number to help you determine each number's value.

Read each number. Write the value of the number in bold on the line.

> **Example:** 3,1**2**4,657.069

> **Answer:** 20,000 or 20 thousands

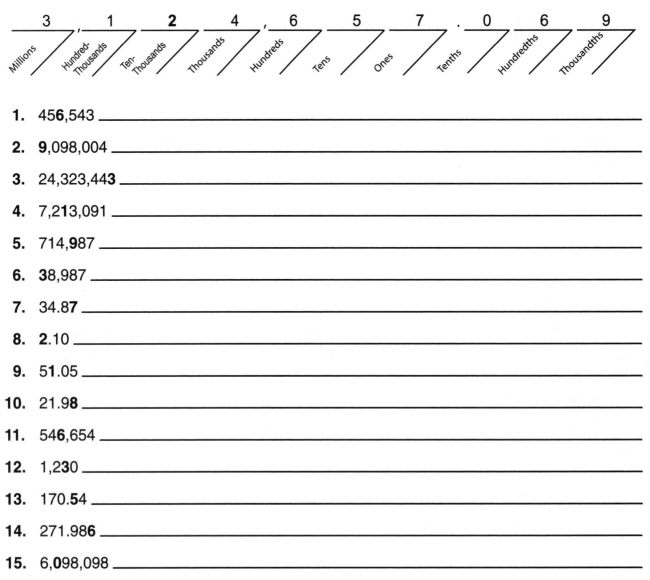

1. 45**6**,543 _____

2. **9**,098,004 _____

3. 24,323,44**3** _____

4. 7,213,091 _____

5. 714,**9**87 _____

6. **3**8,987 _____

7. 34.8**7** _____

8. **2**.10 _____

9. 51.0**5** _____

10. 21.9**8** _____

11. 546,**6**54 _____

12. 1,**2**30 _____

13. 170.**5**4 _____

14. 271.98**6** _____

15. 6,**0**98,098 _____

Name: _____ Date: _____

Skill: Understanding numbers, ways of representing numbers, relationships among numbers, and number systems

Unit 1: Number and Operations: *Practice Activity 3*

Just a Tip: Fractions that are equal are called **equivalent fractions**. Two fractions are equivalent if they can both be reduced to the same fraction.

> **Example:** $\frac{4}{16}$ and $\frac{2}{8}$ $\frac{4}{16} = \frac{1}{4}$ and $\frac{2}{8} = \frac{1}{4}$ These fractions are equivalent.
>
> **Example:** $\frac{1}{2}$ and $\frac{1}{8}$ They are not the same when reduced, so these fractions are NOT equivalent.

Circle the fractions that are equivalent.

1. $\frac{3}{7}, \frac{1}{2}$

2. $\frac{1}{3}, \frac{2}{5}$

3. $\frac{2}{3}, \frac{12}{18}$

4. $\frac{6}{12}, \frac{1}{2}$

5. $\frac{9}{10}, \frac{5}{8}$

6. $\frac{3}{4}, \frac{9}{12}$

7. $\frac{2}{12}, \frac{1}{8}$

8. $\frac{18}{24}, \frac{3}{4}$

Just a Tip: You can find the decimal that is equivalent to a fraction by dividing the numerator by the denominator.

> **Example:** $\frac{7}{20}$ $7 \div 20 = 0.35$ $\frac{7}{20} = 0.35$

Write a decimal that is equivalent to the fraction.

9. $\frac{4}{10}$ _____

10. $3\frac{4}{100}$ _____

11. $5\frac{1}{10}$ _____

12. $\frac{17}{100}$ _____

13. $\frac{8}{10}$ _____

14. $6\frac{25}{50}$ _____

15. $\frac{25}{100}$ _____

Extension Activity: Write ten to twenty fractions on cards. Pass the cards out to students. Have each student draw a picture of the fraction they selected. Then have students look around the room at their classmates' drawings and match equivalent fractions.

5

Name: _____　Date: _____

Skill: Understanding numbers, ways of representing numbers, relationships among numbers, and number systems

Unit 1: Number and Operations: *Practice Activity 4*

< means less than;　　> means greater than;

= means equals

Examples:　1.65 > 1.59　greater than
0.034 < 0.34　less than
0.5 = 0.50　　equals

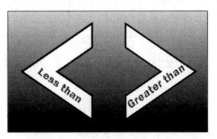

Just a Tip: One way to remember the meaning of the greater than and less than sign is to think in terms of, "I'm bigger than you!" The larger number always points at the smaller number. For example: 1 < 3: The 3 points at the 1 as if saying, "I'm bigger than you!" 7 > 2: The 7 points at the 2 as if saying, "I'm bigger than you!"

Compare each set of decimals. Write <, >, or =.

1.　1.78 _____ 17.87

2.　0.009 _____ 0.09

3.　8.98 _____ 8.89

4.　0.40 _____ 0.04

5.　0.29 _____ 0.78

6.　10.12 _____ 1.012

Write the following numbers in order from least to greatest.

7.　78,989; 45,876; 78,876; 45,987

_____

8.　232,123; 432,342; 235,432; 236,432

_____

9.　98,009; 98,908; 98,008; 89,879

_____

10.　2,343,212; 3,432,123; 234,343; 2,432,432

_____

Write the following numbers in order from greatest to least.

11.　54,323; 55,434; 15,532; 15,232

_____

12.　786,767; 786,878; 786,989; 87,876

_____

13.　132,343; 143,233; 123,123; 144,345

_____

14.　7,987; 7,897; 7,809; 17,876

_____

Name: _____ Date: _____

Skill: Understanding numbers, ways of representing numbers, relationships among numbers, and number systems

Unit 1: Number and Operations: *Assessment 1*

Read each question carefully. Then mark the best answer.

1. Which answer choice represents the number 31,098,987 written in word form?
    ○ A. thirty-one thousand, ninety-eight, nine hundred and eighty-seven
    ○ B. thirty-one million, ninety-eight thousand, nine hundred eighty-seven
    ○ C. thirty-one million, ninety-eight hundred, nine hundred eighty-seven
    ○ D. thirteen million, ninety-eight thousand, nine hundred eighty-seven

2. What is the value of the number in bold?
    40**9**,987
    ○ A. 90,000
    ○ B. 9,000
    ○ C. 900
    ○ D. 90

3. Which number represents the number sixty-nine thousand, seven hundred and five?
    ○ A. 69,075
    ○ B. 69,705
    ○ C. 96,570
    ○ D. 69,715

4. Which answer choice represents the number 234,543 written in word form?
    ○ A. two hundred thirty-four million, five hundred forty-three
    ○ B. two hundred forty-three thousand, five hundred fourteen
    ○ C. two hundred thirty-four thousand, five hundred forty-three
    ○ D. two hundred fourteen thousand, five hundred forty-three

5. Which of the following decimals represents the following: seventeen and seven tenths?
    ○ A. 17.07
    ○ B. 17.7
    ○ C. 1.707
    ○ D. 17.1

6. Which of the following decimals represents the following: twenty-five hundredths?
    ○ A. 0.25
    ○ B. 2.5
    ○ C. 0.025
    ○ D. 2.05

7. What is the value of the number in bold?
    35,**7**86
    ○ A. 6,000
    ○ B. 600
    ○ C. 6
    ○ D. 16

8. What is the value of the number in bold?
    21,**3**23,123
    ○ A. 20,000,000
    ○ B. 2,000,000
    ○ C. 200,000
    ○ D. 2,000

Name: _____ Date: _____

Unit 1: Number and Operations: *Assessment 1 (cont.)*

9. Which of the following fractions is equivalent to $\frac{7}{8}$?

○ A. $\frac{18}{21}$ ○ B. $\frac{12}{20}$ ○ C. $\frac{21}{24}$ ○ D. $\frac{2}{3}$

10. Which answer choice represents the number 9,897,878 in expanded form?
○ A. 9,000,000 + 800,000 + 90,000 + 7,000 + 800 + 70 + 8
○ B. 900,000 + 80,000 + 90,000 + 7,000 + 800 + 70 + 8
○ C. 9,000,000 + 800,000 + 900 + 700 + 800 + 70 + 8
○ D. 9,000,000 + 800,000 + 9,000 + 7,000 + 800 + 70 + 8

11. Which of the following shows the numbers in order from greatest to least?
○ A. 432,321; 432,323; 403,321; 433,232
○ B. 403,321; 432,321; 432,323; 433,232
○ C. 433,232; 432,321; 432,323; 403,321
○ D. 433,232; 432,323; 432,321; 403,321

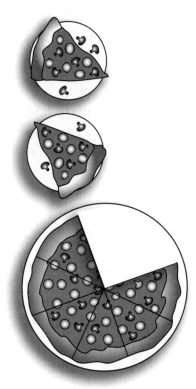

12. Which of the following numbers has the smallest value?
○ A. 124,098
○ B. 32,324
○ C. 32,321
○ D. 32,876

13. Which answer choice represents the number sixteen million, seven hundred eighty-nine thousand, one?
○ A. 61,789,001
○ B. 16,798,001
○ C. 16,789,100
○ D. 16,789,001

14. Which of the following answer choices lists the numbers in order from least to greatest?
○ A. 898,878; 876,876; 897,876; 809,987
○ B. 898,878; 897,876; 876,876; 809,987
○ C. 809,987; 876,876; 897,876; 898,878
○ D. 898,878; 876,876; 897,876; 809,987

15. Which of the following decimals is equivalent to $\frac{1}{2}$?
○ A. 0.075
○ B. 0.050
○ C. 0.50
○ D. 5.0

Name: _____ Date: _____

Skill: Understanding the meanings of operations and how they relate to each other

Unit 1: Number and Operations: *Practice Activity 5*

Mathematical operations are performed in order from left to right, starting with exponents, then multiplication and/or division, and then addition and/or subtraction. Operations inside parentheses are performed first.

Example: $(15 \times 10) \div 5 =$
                     $150 \div 5 = 30$

$(120 \div 12) \times 8 =$
              $10 \times 8 = 80$

Please solve the following fifteen problems. Some of these problems may have remainders. Round answers to the nearest hundredths.

1. $12 \times 8 \div 16 =$ _____

2. $(96 \div 2) \times 4 =$ _____

3. $115 \div 5 \times 3 =$ _____

4. $24 \times 6 \div 4 =$ _____

5. $40 \times 8 \div 12 =$ _____

6. $(50 \times 5) \div 15 =$ _____

7. $135 \div 7 \times 9 =$ _____

8. $16 \times 16 \div 8 =$ _____

9. $156 \div 4 \times 4 =$ _____

10. $174 \div 9 \times 7 =$ _____

11. $140 \times 6 \div 280 =$ _____

12. $(250 \div 2) \times 25 =$ _____

13. $28 \times 8 \div 6 =$ _____

14. $60 \times 12 \div 14 =$ _____

15. $285 \div 6 \times 3 =$ _____

WAKE-UP WORD PROBLEM: Jeremy is delivering packages after school to earn extra money for the holidays. He has eight boxes of packages he needs to deliver during a five-day time period. There are sixteen packages in each box. If Jeremy wants to deliver about the same number of packages each day, approximately how many packages should Jeremy deliver after school each day during the five-day period?

© Mark Twain Media, Inc., Publishers

Name: _____ Date: _____

Skill: Understanding the meanings of operations and how they relate to each other

Unit 1: Number and Operations: *Practice Activity 6*

Read each word problem. On the first line, write the number sentence that should be used to solve the problem. Some of these problems may be two-step problems. Some of these problems may have remainders. On the second line, solve the problem. Look out for key words in each problem. Also think about what the problem is asking so you can be sure to come up with a reasonable answer.

Just a Tip: Here are some key words for **multiplication**: *altogether, in all, groups of.* Here are some key words for **division**: *divided, equal parts, group.*

1. There are 26 classes of grades four through eight at Martin School. There are 18 students in each class. How many total students in grades four through eight attend Martin School?

    _____

    _____

2. Macy is dividing up cookies to sell at the school bake sale. She has a total of 878 cookies. She plans to place three cookies in each bag and sell each bag for $0.25. How many bags of cookies can Macy make?

    _____

    _____

3. Mateo is going to overnight camp for 21 days over the summer. He knows that there are 24 hours in a day. How many hours will Mateo spend at overnight camp?

    _____

    _____

4. Jason and Shane are both on the yearbook staff. They take 776 pictures for the yearbook during the school year. They can only use 138 pictures in the yearbook. The yearbook is 68 pages long. They plan to put the same number of pictures on each page. If they have any extra pictures, they will put them on the last page of the yearbook. How many pictures will Jason and Shane put on each page? How many pictures will they put on the last page?

    _____

    _____

5. Three-thousand, six hundred eighteen people attend a popular rock band's concert. Nine hundred eleven people sit in reserved seating. How many of the people attending the concert do not sit in reserved seating?

    _____

    _____

© Mark Twain Media, Inc., Publishers

Name: _____ Date: _____

Unit 1: Number and Operations: *Practice Activity 6 (cont.)*

6. Jaclyn works at a coffee shop. At the beginning of her eight-hour shift, she makes nine stacks of paper coffee cups next to the coffee machine. She puts ninety-four cups in each stack. How many paper cups does Jaclyn put next to the coffee machine before her shift?

    _____

    _____

7. Jeremiah is in charge of setting up chairs for a large performance Saturday night. He sets up 175 rows of chairs with 92 chairs in each row. How many chairs does Jeremiah set up in all?

    _____

    _____

8. Max eats the same lunch every day during June. He orders a slice of pizza, a garden salad, and a drink for $6.75. The month is thirty days long. How much money does Max spend on lunch during June?

    _____

    _____

9. During summer vacation, Maria answers the phone at a busy law office. During a five-day time period, the law office receives 876 phone calls. Assuming they receive approximately the same number of phone calls each day, how many phone calls does the law office receive each day?

    _____

    _____

10. Lauren compares the mileage on the three family cars. The blue station wagon has 102,657 miles. The red SUV has 16,768 miles more on it than the blue station wagon, and the green truck has 12,987 more miles on it than the red SUV. What is the mileage on the green truck?

    _____

    _____

Extension Activity: Have students look through magazines and select a picture that could represent a multiplication sentence. Have students glue the picture they select on the front of an index card. Then have them write a word problem and a number sentence to go with the picture on the back. You can also have students try this activity with division.

Name: _____   Date: _____

Skill: Understanding the meanings of operations and how they relate to each other

Unit 1: Number and Operations: *Practice Activity 7*

Just a Tip: In the **Commutative Property of Multiplication**, the order of the factors does not change the product. In the **Associative Property of Multiplication**, the way the factors are grouped does not change the product. Remember, do the work in parentheses first!

Multiplication and division are **inverse operations**, just like addition and subtraction. This means that multiplication undoes division, and division undoes multiplication.

Commutative Property of Multiplication

Use the Commutative Property to write a different multiplication sentence that results in the same product for each of the following number sentences.

1. 7 x 6 = _____   4. 9 x 9 = _____
2. 84 x 6 = _____   5. 12 x 15 = _____
3. 20 x 5 = _____

Associative Property of Multiplication

Use the Associative Property to multiply three factors. If necessary, use the Commutative Property to change the order.

6. (18 x 4) x 6 = _____   11. 25 x (40 x 2) = _____
7. (5 x 9) x 10 = _____   12. 8 x (7 x 4) = _____
8. 13 x (15 x 8) = _____   13. (9 x 9) x 24 = _____
9. (24 x 8) x 3 = _____   14. (14 x 7) x 5 = _____
10. (16 x 10) x 5 = _____   15. 5 x (15 x 12) = _____

Look at the following number sentences. Write an inverse operation on the line below each problem.

16. 18 ÷ 6 = _____   19. 100 x 4 = _____
17. 12 x 5 = _____   20. 110 ÷ 10 = _____
18. 64 ÷ 2 = _____

WAKE-UP WORD PROBLEM: Mia buys a large container of lollipops to sell at the school store. The large container of lollipops cost Mia $7.75. There are 215 lollipops in the large container. The lollipops are sold at the school store for $0.25 each. How much money will the large container of lollipops Mia purchased earn for the store after the price of the lollipops is deducted?

_____

Name: _____   Date: _____

Skill: Understanding the meanings of operations and how they relate to each other

Unit 1: Number and Operations: *Assessment 2*

Mark the best answer for the following problems.

1. 12 x 5 ÷ 4 =
    - ○ A. 10
    - ○ B. 5
    - ○ C. 15
    - ○ D. 4

2. 90 x 10 ÷ 9 =
    - ○ A. 40
    - ○ B. 60
    - ○ C. 100
    - ○ D. 80

Mark the answer that shows the correct number sentence to solve the problem.

3. Pierre calculates that he will spend $17.25 each day he is on vacation with his family. He will be on vacation with his family for 15 days. Approximately how much money will Pierre spend in all while he is on vacation?
    - ○ A. $17.25 ÷ 15 =
    - ○ B. $258.75 ÷ 15 =
    - ○ C. 15 x $12.75 =
    - ○ D. $17.25 x 15 =

4. Leroy drives 344 miles during a two-day period. Assuming he drives the same number of miles each day, how many miles does Leroy drive each day?
    - ○ A. 344 x 2 =
    - ○ B. 2 ÷ 344 =
    - ○ C. 344 ÷ 2 =
    - ○ D. 344 + 344 =

5. Sarah Lee orders 776 chairs for the auditorium. Ninety-seven of the chairs are made of oak, and the remaining chairs are made of pine. How many of the chairs that Sarah Lee orders are made of pine?
    - ○ A. 776 - 97 =
    - ○ B. 776 ÷ 2 =
    - ○ C. 97 x 776 =
    - ○ D. 776 ÷ 97 =

Name: _____　Date: _____

Unit 1: Number and Operations: *Assessment 2 (cont.)*

Mark the answer that solves the problem.

6. (64 x 2) x 6 =
- ○ A. 678
- ○ B. 768
- ○ C. 788
- ○ D. 748

7. 14 x (14 x 10) =
- ○ A. 2,800
- ○ B. 2,140
- ○ C. 1,960
- ○ D. 1,730

8. (8 x 9) x 11 =
- ○ A. 721
- ○ B. 891
- ○ C. 792
- ○ D. 746

Mark the answer that shows an example of an inverse operation.

9. 40 ÷ 8 =
- ○ A. 40 ÷ 5 =
- ○ B. 40 x 8 =
- ○ C. 4 x 10 =
- ○ D. 8 x 5 =

10. 32 ÷ 2 =
- ○ A. 16 x 2 =
- ○ B. 32 ÷ 4 =
- ○ C. 4 x 8 =
- ○ D. 32 ÷ 16 =

11. 12 x 11 =
- ○ A. 11 x 12 =
- ○ B. 132 ÷ 12 =
- ○ C. 12 x 12 =
- ○ D. 132 ÷ 2 =

Mark the answer for the number that is missing in the number sentence.

12. 56 ÷ ___ = 14
- ○ A. 2
- ○ B. 5
- ○ C. 4
- ○ D. 6

13. 21 x ___ = 105
- ○ A. 8
- ○ B. 5
- ○ C. 6
- ○ D. 7

Mark the answer for the sign that needs to be added to solve each problem.

14. 550 ___ 5 = 110
- ○ A. +
- ○ B. -
- ○ C. x
- ○ D. ÷

15. 12 ___ 9 = 108
- ○ A. +
- ○ B. -
- ○ C. x
- ○ D. ÷

Name: _____   Date: _____

Skill: Computing fluently and making reasonable estimates

Unit 1: Number and Operations: *Practice Activity 8*

Estimates can be made by rounding the numbers before performing the operation.

Just a Tip: Making reasonable estimates with numbers with zeros is easy. Look at the problem 400 x 300. First, multiply the numbers 4 x 3 (= 12). Then add the number of zeros in the problem (four zeros total on 400 and 300). So, the correct answer is 120,000.

Multiply the following rounded numbers.

1. 300 x 600 = _____
2. 100 x 200 = _____
3. 400 x 100 = _____
4. 700 x 500 = _____
5. 500 x 500 = _____
6. 300 x 200 = _____
7. 80 x 400 = _____
8. 900 x 200 = _____
9. 30 x 300 = _____
10. 40 x 500 = _____
11. 1,000 x 90 = _____
12. 80 x 8,000 = _____
13. 700 x 40 = _____
14. 3,000 x 50 = _____
15. 20 x 200 = _____
16. 60 x 600 = _____
17. 10 x 8,000 = _____
18. 40 x 900 = _____
19. 2,000 x 500 = _____
20. 900 x 7,000 = _____

WAKE-UP WORD PROBLEM: About 700 people visit the carnival every night from Monday through Saturday. About how many total people visit the carnival from Monday through Saturday?

_____

© Mark Twain Media, Inc., Publishers   15

Name: _____ Date: _____

Skill: Computing fluently and making reasonable estimates

Unit 1: Number and Operations: *Practice Activity 9*

When rounding numbers, look at the number to the immediate right of the place you are rounding to. If the number to the right is 5 or more, round up. If the number to the right is 4 or less, round down.

Examples: Rounding to the nearest thousand, **5,921 = 6,000** and **5,375 = 5,000**.
Rounding to the nearest ten, **347 = 350** and **682 = 680**.

Round each number to the nearest thousand.

1. 17,876	_____		**4.** 555,543	_____
2. 24,345	_____		**5.** 10,654	_____
3. 232,654	_____		**6.** 316,472	_____

Round each number to the nearest ten thousand.

7. 66,342	_____		**10.** 87,876	_____
8. 235,432	_____		**11.** 91,765	_____
9. 131,432	_____		**12.** 652,190	_____

Round each number to the nearest hundred thousand.

13. 543,876	_____		**16.** 654,343	_____
14. 2,343,876	_____		**17.** 5,786,876	_____
15. 897,866	_____		**18.** 1,092,116	_____

Round each number to the nearest million.

19. 32,232,234	_____		**23.** 21,654,876	_____
20. 1,878,987	_____		**24.** 10,781,237	_____
21. 2,000,000	_____		**25.** 6,283,999	_____
22. 3,432,776	_____			

Extension Activity: Have students find numbers in the newspaper and/or reference materials and round them to a given place.

Name: _____ Date: _____

Skill: Computing fluently and making reasonable estimates

Unit 1: Number and Operations: *Practice Activity 10*

Read each word problem. First, round each number. Then determine the best estimate of the answer. Finally, write a complete sentence that gives the answer to the word problem. The first one is done as an example.

1. Tina spends $167 at the grocery store one week and $112 at the grocery store the next week. About how much money does Tina spend at the grocery store during two weeks? (Round to the nearest hundred.)

   $200 + $100 = $300

   Tina spends about $300 at the grocery store in two weeks.

2. Rice and Roll Restaurant recycled 787 cans during May and 212 fewer cans during June. About how many total cans did Rice and Roll Restaurant recycle during May and June? (Round to the nearest hundred.)

   _____

   _____

3. Melanie and Rod go swimming 12 times each month during a six-month period. About how many times do Melanie and Rod swim during a six-month period? (Round to the nearest ten.)

   _____

   _____

4. Terri compares the cost of a milkshake at three ice cream shops around town. The costs are as follows: $3.56, $2.19 and $2.89. What is the average cost of a chocolate milkshake in town? (Round to the nearest dollar.)

   _____

   _____

5. The enrollment at Happy Hills Summer Camp is 1,878 campers during the 2002–2003 season and 1,045 campers during the 2003–2004 season. About how many campers attend Happy Hills Summer Camp during both years combined? (Round to the nearest thousand.)

   _____

   _____

Name: _____ Date: _____

Unit 1: Number and Operations: *Practice Activity 10 (cont.)*

6. Tyrone and Theresa record the number of times they go out to eat during a six-month period. They go out to eat 24 times during May, 18 times during June, 16 times during July, 27 times during August, 33 times during September, and 41 times during October. About how many times on average do they eat out each month? (Round to the nearest ten.)

_____

_____

7. Tara has 314 stickers in her sticker collection. Her sister has 479 stickers in her collection. About how many more stickers does Tara's sister have in her collection? (Round to the nearest hundred.)

_____

_____

8. The three elementary schools in the Steiner Elementary School District record their enrollment. The enrollment at each elementary school is as follows: 1,234; 2,001; 2,333. About how many total students are enrolled in all three elementary schools? (Round to the nearest thousand.)

_____

_____

9. Sam's family goes out to dinner on Friday night. They each order an entrée. Sam and his sister each order a hamburger for $5.50. His dad orders a steak for $9.25 and his mom orders a baked potato for $3.95. About how much does Sam's family spend on dinner? (Round to the nearest dollar.)

_____

_____

Name: _____ Date: _____

Skill: Computing fluently and making reasonable estimates

Unit 1: Number and Operations: *Assessment 3*

Follow the directions above each problem. Then mark the best answer to the problem.

Round each number to the nearest thousand.

1. 17,765
   - A. 17,000
   - B. 17,500
   - C. 18,000
   - D. 18,900

2. 21,546
   - A. 21,500
   - B. 22,000
   - C. 21,000
   - D. 19,000

Round each number to the nearest ten thousand.

3. 54,321
   - A. 54,000
   - B. 50,000
   - C. 60,000
   - D. 51,000

4. 213,654
   - A. 200,000
   - B. 215,000
   - C. 213,000
   - D. 210,000

Round each number to the nearest hundred thousand.

5. 678,987
   - A. 675,000
   - B. 700,000
   - C. 678,000
   - D. 600,000

6. 323,987
   - A. 320,098
   - B. 300,000
   - C. 320,000
   - D. 400,000

Round each number to the nearest million.

7. 12,987,987
   - A. 12,000,000
   - B. 13,000,000
   - C. 12,900,000
   - D. 12,988,000

8. 4,565,234
   - A. 4,500,000
   - B. 4,000,000
   - C. 5,000,000
   - D. 5,500,000

Round each answer to the nearest thousand.

9. 17,765 - 11,009 =
   - A. 6,700
   - B. 6,750
   - C. 6,000
   - D. 7,000

10. 51,009 - 22,345 =
   - A. 29,000
   - B. 28,000
   - C. 30,000
   - D. 35,000

Name: _____ Date: _____

Unit 1: Number and Operations: *Assessment 3 (cont.)*

Round each answer to the nearest ten thousand.

11. 55,764 + 31,002 =
○ A. 85,000
○ B. 86,000
○ C. 86,700
○ D. 90,000

12. 192,543 - 79,801 =
○ A. 120,000
○ B. 125,000
○ C. 110,000
○ D. 90,000

Round each answer to the nearest million.

13. 72,865,213 + 1,045,967 =
○ A. 74,000,000
○ B. 73,000,000
○ C. 72,000,000
○ D. 75,000,000

14. 8,892,611 - 6,701,538 =
○ A. 1,000,000
○ B. 3,000,000
○ C. 14,000,000
○ D. 2,000,000

Compute mentally to solve the following problems.

15. 800 x 900 =
○ A. 720,000
○ B. 72,000
○ C. 7,200
○ D. 77,000

16. 2,000 x 300 =
○ A. 60,000
○ B. 6,000
○ C. 600,000
○ D. 6,000,000

17. 500 x 500 =
○ A. 250
○ B. 2,500,000
○ C. 25,000
○ D. 250,000

18. 40 x 20,000 =
○ A. 8,000
○ B. 800
○ C. 800,000
○ D. 80,000

19. 7,000 x 800 =
○ A. 5,600
○ B. 5,600,000
○ C. 56,000
○ D. 560,000

20. 900 x 30 =
○ A. 270
○ B. 2,700
○ C. 27,000
○ D. 270,000

Review of Three Previously Taught NCTM Standards

- **Understanding numbers, ways of representing numbers, relationships among numbers, and number systems**

- **Understanding meanings of operations and how they relate to each other**

- **Computing fluently and making reasonable estimates**

Mark the best answer choice.

1. Which of the following represents the number 6,098,999 in expanded form?
    - ○ A. 6,000,000 + 90,000 + 80,000 + 900 + 90 + 9 =
    - ○ B. 600,000 + 900,000 + 80,000 + 900 + 99 =
    - ○ C. 6,000,000 + 900,000 + 80,000 + 900 + 90 + 9 =
    - ○ D. 6,000,000 + 90,000 + 8,000 + 900 + 90 + 9 =

2. Which of the following represents the number 209,887 in written form?
    - ○ A. two hundred and ninety thousand, eight hundred and eighty-seven
    - ○ B. two hundred nine thousand, eight hundred eighty-seven
    - ○ C. two hundred ninety thousand, eight hundred eighty-seven
    - ○ D. two hundred nine thousand, eight hundred seven

3. What is the value of the number in bold 78,9**8**7,876?
    - ○ A. 80,000
    - ○ B. 800,000
    - ○ C. 8,000
    - ○ D. 18,000

4. Which of the following shows the numbers in order from greatest to least?
    - ○ A. 345,237; 345,234; 345,098; 305,098; 314,323
    - ○ B. 305,098; 314,323; 345,098; 345,234; 345,237
    - ○ C. 345,237; 345,234; 345,098; 314,323; 305,098
    - ○ D. 345,237; 345,234; 314,323; 345,098; 305,098

5. Solve the problem: 32 x 4 ÷ 6 =
    - ○ A. 21 remainder 2
    - ○ B. 21 remainder 3
    - ○ C. 22
    - ○ D. 24

Name: _____ Date: _____

Review of Three Previously Taught NCTM Standards (cont.)

6. Lauren takes $72.50 on her sponsored band trip to New Orleans, Louisiana. The trip will last a total of eight days. Lauren spends an equal amount of money during each of the eight days. Approximately how much money does Lauren spend each day?
   - ○ A. $8.03
   - ○ B. $9.03
   - ○ C. $9.10
   - ○ D. $9.06

7. Use the associative property to multiply the three factors: (7 x 17) x 128 =
   - ○ A. 12,232
   - ○ B. 15,204
   - ○ C. 15,232
   - ○ D. 15,236

8. Round the number 1,232,009 to the nearest ten thousand.
   - ○ A. 1,235,000
   - ○ B. 1,230,000
   - ○ C. 1,300,000
   - ○ D. 1,200,000

9. Round the answer to the problem to the nearest hundred thousand.
   342,453 - 128,989 =
   - ○ A. 212,000
   - ○ B. 210,000
   - ○ C. 200,000
   - ○ D. 300,000

10. Round the number 55,342,789 to the nearest million.
    - ○ A. 55,350,000
    - ○ B. 55,300,000
    - ○ C. 60,000,000
    - ○ D. 55,000,000

11. Which of the following shows the numbers in order from least to greatest?
    - ○ A. 1,232,432; 1,323,432; 1,300,009; 1,234,321
    - ○ B. 1,323,432; 1,300,009; 1,234,321; 1,232,432
    - ○ C. 1,232,432; 1,234,321; 1,323,432; 1,300,009
    - ○ D. 1,232,432; 1,234,321; 1,300,009; 1,323,432

12. Which sign should be added to make the following number sentence true?
    75 ___ 181 = 13,575
    - ○ A. +
    - ○ B. -
    - ○ C. x
    - ○ D. ÷

13. Use the Associative Property to multiply the following three factors.
    545 x 65 x 8 =
    - ○ A. 28,340,000
    - ○ B. 283,400
    - ○ C. 287,400
    - ○ D. 2,830,400

14. Which sign should be added to make the following number sentence true?
    98.75 ___ 97.85
    - ○ A. >
    - ○ B. <
    - ○ C. =

15. Which sign should be added to make the following number sentence true?
    105.02 ___ 105.020
    - ○ A. >
    - ○ B. <
    - ○ C. =

Name: _____   Date: _____

Skill: Understanding patterns, relations, and functions

Unit 2: Algebra: *Practice Activity 1*

Complete the following numeric patterns.

Look for a number pattern in each sequence. It might help to record what the pattern is above or below each number.

Example: 2, 6, 18, 54, 162, 486
            x3 x3 x3 x3 x3

1. 131, 119, _____, 95, 83, _____, _____

2. 8, 32, _____, 512, _____, _____, 32,768

3. _____, _____, 119, 138, 157, _____, 195

4. 239, 230, 221, _____, _____, 194, 185

5. 18, 36, 72, _____, 288, 576, _____

6. 9, 27, _____, _____, 81, _____, 117

7. _____, 74, 90, _____, _____, 138, 154

8. 12, 39, _____, _____, 120, 147, _____

Fill in the missing letters.

9. A, D, _____, J, _____, _____

10. X, W, U, T, _____, _____, O

11. G, H, J, K, _____, _____, _____, Q

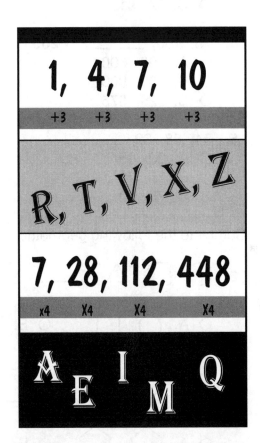

12. Look at the following three flight schedules. Based on the patterns on each flight schedule, fill in the missing arrival and departure dates and flight number.

Daily Flight Schedule between New York City and Chicago, Illinois		
Flight #	Departure Time	Arrival Time
13	6:44 A.M.	_____
19	9:55 A.M.	12:57 P.M.
25	_____	5:03 P.M.
31	_____	8:17 P.M.
_____	9:03 P.M.	

Name: _____   Date: _____

Skill: Understanding patterns, relations, and functions

Unit 2: Algebra: *Practice Activity 2*

Complete the following numeric patterns and mark the best answer for each.

1. 82, 73, ___, ___, 46, 37
   - ○ A. 65, 56
   - ○ B. 64, 55
   - ○ C. 82, 91

2. 2, 4, 8, ___, 32, ___
   - ○ A. 10, 24
   - ○ B. 18, 65
   - ○ C. 16, 64

3. 75, 150, ___, ___, 1,200
   - ○ A. 300, 600
   - ○ B. 600, 900
   - ○ C. 325, 675

4. 17, 38, 59, ___, ___
   - ○ A. 80, 101
   - ○ B. 38, 17
   - ○ C. 81, 102

5. 94, 88, 82, ___, ___
   - ○ A. 89, 95
   - ○ B. 75, 71
   - ○ C. 76, 70

Complete the following geometric patterns and/or letter patterns.

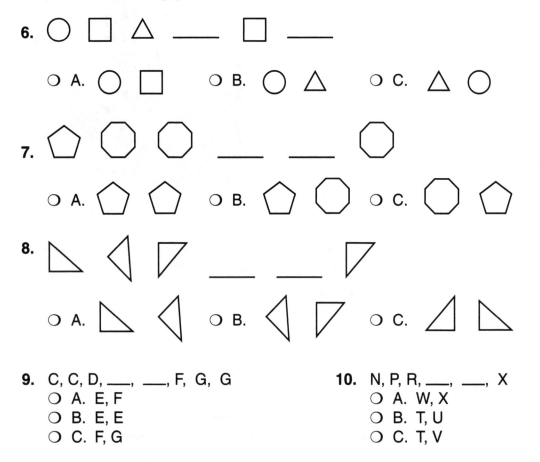

9. C, C, D, ___, ___, F, G, G
   - ○ A. E, F
   - ○ B. E, E
   - ○ C. F, G

10. N, P, R, ___, ___, X
   - ○ A. W, X
   - ○ B. T, U
   - ○ C. T, V

© Mark Twain Media, Inc., Publishers

Name: _____ Date: _____

Unit 2: Algebra: *Practice Activity 2 (cont.)*

Based on the pattern shown, fill in the flight schedule, and then answer the following questions about the flight schedule.

Daily Non-Stop Flight between Seattle, Washington, and Anchorage, Alaska

Flight #	Departure Time:	Arrival Time:
54	7:22 A.M.	10:22 A.M.
49	10:15 A.M.	_____
__	2:00 P.M.	_____
39	_____	5:00 P.M.
34	_____	9:20 P.M.

---

11. Based on the pattern on the schedule, what time will flight #49 arrive in Anchorage, Alaska?
    - ○ A. 1:22 P.M.
    - ○ B. 1:15 P.M.
    - ○ C. 12:15 P.M.

12. Based on the pattern on the schedule, what is the number(s) for the flight that departs Seattle, Washington, at 2:00 P.M.?
    - ○ A. #44 and #39
    - ○ B. #45 and #39
    - ○ C. #40

13. Based on the pattern on the schedule, what time will the flights that leave Seattle, Washington, at 2:00 P.M. arrive in Anchorage, Alaska?
    - ○ A. 6:00 P.M.
    - ○ B. 4:40 P.M.
    - ○ C. 5:00 P.M.

14. Based on the pattern on the schedule, what time will flight #39 leave Seattle, Washington?
    - ○ A. 8:00 P.M.
    - ○ B. 2:00 P.M.
    - ○ C. 3:15 P.M.

15. Based on the pattern on the schedule, what time will flight #34 leave Seattle, Washington?
    - ○ A. 2:00 P.M.
    - ○ B. 10:15 A.M.
    - ○ C. 6:20 P.M.

© Mark Twain Media, Inc., Publishers

Name: _____   Date: _____

Skill: Understanding patterns, relations, and functions

Unit 2: Algebra: *Assessment 1*

Read the directions above each problem. Then mark the best answer.

Fill in the missing numbers or letters in each pattern.

1. 96, 87, _____, _____, 60, _____

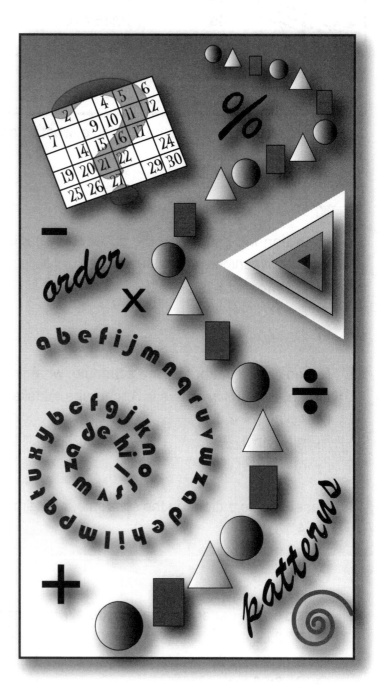

- ○ A. 77, 70, 52
- ○ B. 78, 69, 51
- ○ C. 79, 70, 52
- ○ D. 105, 114, 123

2. 6, 12, _____, _____, 96

- ○ A. 36, 64
- ○ B. 24, 45
- ○ C. 25, 50
- ○ D. 24, 48

3. 365, _____, 337, 323, _____

- ○ A. 351, 309
- ○ B. 350, 310
- ○ C. 371, 385
- ○ D. 321, 395

4. Y, V, _____, _____, M

- ○ A. X, N
- ○ B. S, P
- ○ C. P, W
- ○ D. V, W

5. _____, D, F, _____, _____

- ○ A. B, I, J
- ○ B. B, H, J
- ○ C. A, H, J
- ○ D. C, E, G

Name: _____   Date: _____

Unit 2: Algebra: *Assessment 1 (cont.)*

Fill in the missing times on the schedule. Please use the chart to solve problems 6–9.

Daily Trolley Schedule between Uptown and Midtown		
Trolley #	**Leave Uptown**	**Arrive Midtown**
40	9:06 A.M.	_____
51	9:21 A.M.	9:39 A.M.
62	10:17 A.M.	_____
73	_____	10:44 A.M.
84	12:08 P.M.	_____

6. Based on the pattern on the schedule, what time will Trolley #40 arrive Midtown?
  ○ A. 9:12 A.M.
  ○ B. 9:44 A.M.
  ○ C. 9:24 A.M.
  ○ D. 9:29 A.M.

7. Based on the pattern on the schedule, what time will Trolley #62 arrive Midtown?
  ○ A. 10:35 A.M.
  ○ B. 10:36 A.M.
  ○ C. 10:28 A.M.
  ○ D. 11:21 A.M.

8. Based on the pattern on the schedule, what time will Trolley #73 leave Uptown?
  ○ A. 10:26 A.M.
  ○ B. 9:24 A.M.
  ○ C. 9:26 A.M.
  ○ D. 11:21 A.M.

9. Based on the pattern on the schedule, what time will Trolley #84 arrive Midtown?
  ○ A. 11:26 P.M
  ○ B. 12:18 P.M
  ○ C. 12:24 P.M
  ○ D. 12:26 P.M

Extension Activity: Look for patterns in your everyday life. Record some of the patterns you find on the lines below.

_____

_____

Name: _____ Date: _____

Skill: Representing and analyzing mathematical situations and structures using algebraic symbols

Unit 2: Algebra: *Practice Activity 3*

A **variable** is a letter that stands for an unknown number. ***Example:*** $20 \div n = 5$ $n = 4$
To solve for the unknown number represented by the variable, perform the inverse operation. Using the example above ($20 \div n = 5$), ask, "What number, multiplied by 5, will equal 20?" The answer is **4**.

Fill in the unknown number represented by the variable.

1. $7 \times y = 105$ _____

2. $14 \times r = 84$ _____

3. $49 \div x = 7$ _____

4. $180 \div b = 60$ _____

5. $297 - y = 154$ _____

6. $3,765 - a = 219$ _____

7. $450 \div c = 90$ _____

8. $y \times 33 = 330$ _____

9. $23 \times r = 368$ _____

10. $7,987 - c = 501$ _____

11. $2,123 + n = 3,001$ _____

12. $2,112 \div t = 352$ _____

Use <, >, or = to fill in each number sentence.

13. 234,543 ____ 2,001,098

14. 23,432 ____ 23,004

15. 87,080 ____ 87,808

16. 0.809 ____ 0.890

17. 77.03 ____ 77.030

18. 921.542 ____ 912.542

19. 504,922 ____ 54,902

20. 269.510 ____ 269.51

WAKE-UP WORD PROBLEM: Jacob is buying holiday presents for his three sisters. He spends $7.65 on a present for Molly, $8.01 on a present for Sarah, and $9.75 on a present for Cara. He has $17.61 left over after he purchases all three presents. How much money did Jacob have before he bought holiday presents?

Name: _____ Date: _____

Skill: Representing and analyzing mathematical situations and structure using algebraic symbols

Unit 2: Algebra: *Practice Activity 4*

Just a Tip: The variable represents the missing number in each sentence. For example, in **6 + b = 12**, **b** is the missing number. It is the variable.

Mark the answer that is represented by the variable.

1. $31 \times b = 279$
- ○ A. 8
- ○ B. 9
- ○ C. 6
- ○ D. 8

2. $344 - r = 173$
- ○ A. 171
- ○ B. 117
- ○ C. 170
- ○ D. 172

3. $1,498 + 709 = x$
- ○ A. 1,098
- ○ B. 2,107
- ○ C. 2,207
- ○ D. 789

4. $80 \div n = 8$
- ○ A. 4
- ○ B. 5
- ○ C. 10
- ○ D. 8

5. $87 \times y = 1,392$
- ○ A. 14
- ○ B. 12
- ○ C. 16
- ○ D. 18

6. $18 \times r = 432$
- ○ A. 24
- ○ B. 25
- ○ C. 21
- ○ D. 18

7. $7,008 - x = 6,919$
- ○ A. 88
- ○ B. 89
- ○ C. 87
- ○ D. 85

8. $580 \div c = 116$
- ○ A. 5
- ○ B. 6
- ○ C. 7
- ○ D. 4

9. $27,654 - m = 27,455$
- ○ A. 198
- ○ B. 199
- ○ C. 178
- ○ D. 109

Mark the symbol that makes each number sentence true.

10. 10,001 _____ 10,100
- ○ A. >
- ○ B. <
- ○ C. =

11. 78,987 _____ 78,887
- ○ A. >
- ○ B. <
- ○ C. =

12. 21.32 _____ 21.320
- ○ A. >
- ○ B. <
- ○ C. =

13. 9,098,098 _____ 9,009,089
- ○ A. >
- ○ B. <
- ○ C. =

14. 7.809 _____ 7.890
- ○ A. >
- ○ B. <
- ○ C. =

15. 32.009 _____ 32.06
- ○ A. >
- ○ B. <
- ○ C. =

Name: _____ Date: _____

Skill: Representing and analyzing mathematical situations and structure using algebraic symbols

Unit 2: Algebra: Assessment 2

Mark the answer that is represented by the variable.

1. $91 \times y = 1{,}729$
   - ○ A. 19
   - ○ B. 18
   - ○ C. 17
   - ○ D. 15

2. $798 \div r = 399$
   - ○ A. 2
   - ○ B. 3
   - ○ C. 4
   - ○ D. 6

3. $56{,}098 - s = 56{,}081$
   - ○ A. 17
   - ○ B. 71
   - ○ C. 18
   - ○ D. 21

4. $160 \div x = 40$
   - ○ A. 2
   - ○ B. 4
   - ○ C. 6
   - ○ D. 8

5. $21{,}987 + b = 33{,}990$
   - ○ A. 12,003
   - ○ B. 12,300
   - ○ C. 12,030
   - ○ D. 21,003

6. $41 \times b = 697$
   - ○ A. 14
   - ○ B. 17
   - ○ C. 16
   - ○ D. 18

7. $50 \times 50 = c$
   - ○ A. 2,000
   - ○ B. 2,500
   - ○ C. 1,500
   - ○ D. 1,800

8. $1{,}240 \div x = 310$
   - ○ A. 2
   - ○ B. 3
   - ○ C. 4
   - ○ D. 6

9. $25{,}007 - n = 7{,}004$
   - ○ A. 18,313
   - ○ B. 18,303
   - ○ C. 18,003
   - ○ D. 18,213

Mark the answer for the sign that makes each number sentence true.

10. 740,872 _____ 704,987
    - ○ A. >
    - ○ B. <
    - ○ C. =

11. 56.768 _____ 56.087
    - ○ A. >
    - ○ B. <
    - ○ C. =

12. 10,009 _____ 10,909
    - ○ A. >
    - ○ B. <
    - ○ C. =

13. 99.010 _____ 99.01
    - ○ A. >
    - ○ B. <
    - ○ C. =

14. 8,876,987 _____ 8,789,009
    - ○ A. >
    - ○ B. <
    - ○ C. =

15. 975 _____ 905
    - ○ A. >
    - ○ B. <
    - ○ C. =

© Mark Twain Media, Inc., Publishers

Name: _____ Date: _____

Skill: Analyzing the characteristics and properties of two- and three-dimensional geometric shapes, and developing mathematical arguments about geometric relationships

Unit 3: Geometry: *Practice Activity 1*

Look at each shape. Using the words in the box, write the name that describes each shape on the line. Not all words will be used.

| cylinder | cone | cube | hexagon | triangular prism |
| sphere | pyramid | octagon | rectangle | rectangular prism |

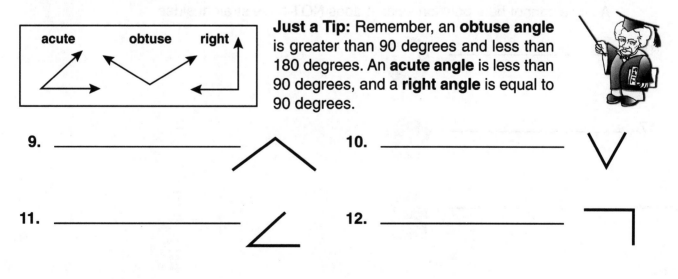

1. _____

2. _____

3. _____

4. _____

5. _____

6. _____

7. _____

8. _____

Look at each angle. Use your estimation skills. Decide if each angle is an acute angle, right angle or obtuse angle.

Just a Tip: Remember, an **obtuse angle** is greater than 90 degrees and less than 180 degrees. An **acute angle** is less than 90 degrees, and a **right angle** is equal to 90 degrees.

acute   obtuse   right

9. _____

10. _____

11. _____

12. _____

Name: _____ Date: _____

Unit 3: Geometry: *Practice Activity 1 (cont.)*

Look at all five pictures. Circle the two figures that are congruent.

Just a Tip: Congruent means same size, same shape. Look for the two shapes that are the same size and shape.

13.

14.   A   E   V   A   F

15.

A **polygon** is a two-dimensional figure that has straight sides. Look at each figure below. Write the word "polygon" next to each of the shapes that is a polygon. Leave the lines next to the shape blank if the shape is not a polygon.

Just a Tip: A polygon must have straight sides. **Example:**

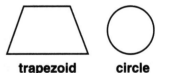

trapezoid   circle
(polygon)   (not a polygon)

A circle cannot be a polygon since it does NOT have straight sides.

16. _____ O

17. _____ ⬠

18. _____ B

© Mark Twain Media, Inc., Publishers

Name: _____ Date: _____

**Skill: Analyzing the characteristics and properties of two- and three-dimensional geo-
metric shapes, and developing mathematical arguments about geometric relationships**

Unit 3: Geometry: *Practice Activity 2*

An **obtuse triangle** has one obtuse angle; this angle measures greater than 90
degrees but less than 180 degrees.
An **acute triangle** has three acute angles; each angle measures less than 90
degrees.
A **right triangle** has one right angle; this angle measures 90 degrees and forms
a square corner.
An **isosceles triangle** has at least two sides that are equal.
An **equilateral triangle** has three angles and sides that are equal.
A **scalene triangle** does not have any sides or angles that are equal.

Circle the word that best describes each triangle.

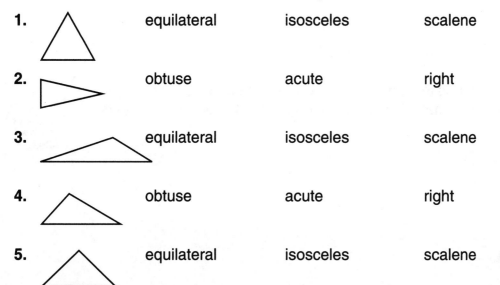

1.   equilateral   isosceles   scalene

2.   obtuse   acute   right

3.   equilateral   isosceles   scalene

4.   obtuse   acute   right

5.   equilateral   isosceles   scalene

Circle the word that best describes each three-dimensional shape.

6.   cube   sphere   cylinder

7.   cylinder   cube   rectangular prism

8.   pyramid   cube   rectangular prism

© Mark Twain Media, Inc., Publishers   33

Name: _____ Date: _____

Unit 3: Geometry: *Practice Activity 2 (cont.)*

Mark the answer for the shape that is congruent to the shape in the box.

Just a Tip: Congruency means same size, same shape.

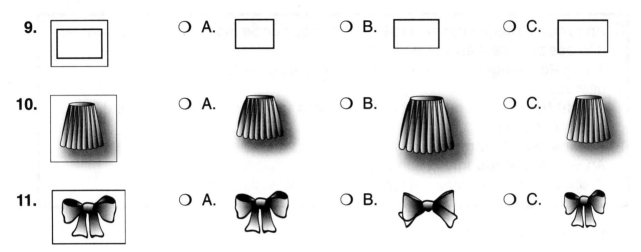

9.   ○ A.   ○ B.   ○ C.

10.   ○ A.   ○ B.   ○ C.

11.   ○ A.   ○ B.   ○ C.

For each pair below, circle the letter that has a line of symmetry.

Just a Tip: Symmetry means that one side reflects the other. For example, look at the heart. The line of symmetry is drawn down the middle. One side reflects the other.

Example:

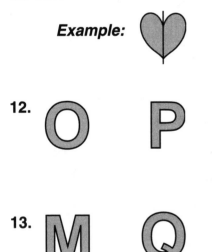

12.   O   P

13.   M   Q

© Mark Twain Media, Inc., Publishers

Name: _____ Date: _____

Unit 3: Geometry: *Practice Activity 2 (cont.)*

Read the definition for each of the following types of triangles. Then write the word that best identifies the triangle on the line.

Isosceles triangle: has at least two sides that are equal
Equilateral triangle: has three angles and sides that are equal
Scalene triangle: does not have any sides or angles that are equal

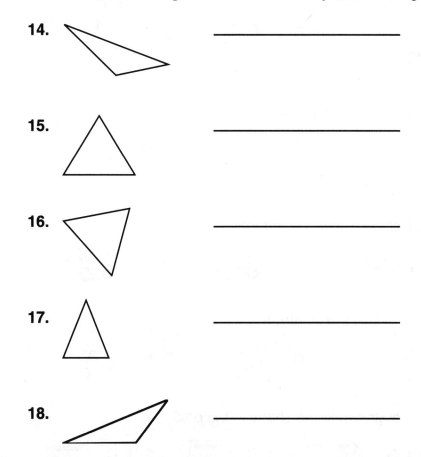

14. _____

15. _____

16. _____

17. _____

18. _____

WAKE-UP WORD PROBLEM: Laura collects boxes of pencils for the Back-to-School Drive in her neighborhood. She collects 718 boxes of pencils. There are 24 pencils in each box. What is the total number of pencils that Laura collects for the Back-to-School Drive?

_____

E x t e n s i o n   A c t i v i t y : Look through magazines and newspapers for symmetrical shapes. Use a marker or dark pencil to draw one or more lines of symmetry on each shape.

Name: _____ Date: _____

Skill: Analyzing the characteristics and properties of two- and three-dimensional geometric shapes, and developing mathematical arguments about geometric relationships

Unit 3: Geometry: *Assessment 1*

Read each problem carefully. Then mark the best answer choice.

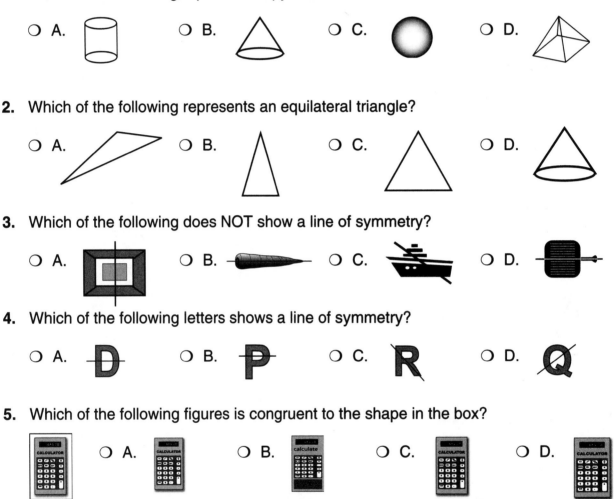

1. Which of the following represents a pyramid?

    ○ A.   ○ B.   ○ C.   ○ D.

2. Which of the following represents an equilateral triangle?

    ○ A.   ○ B.   ○ C.   ○ D.

3. Which of the following does NOT show a line of symmetry?

    ○ A.   ○ B.   ○ C.   ○ D.

4. Which of the following letters shows a line of symmetry?

    ○ A. D   ○ B. P   ○ C. R   ○ D. Q

5. Which of the following figures is congruent to the shape in the box?

    ○ A.   ○ B.   ○ C.   ○ D.

6. Look at the triangle in the box. Mark the answer that best describes the triangle.

    ○ A. scalene, right
    ○ B. obtuse, scalene
    ○ C. right
    ○ D. scalene

Name: _____ Date: _____

Unit 3: Geometry: *Assessment 1 (cont.)*

7. Which of the following is a right triangle?

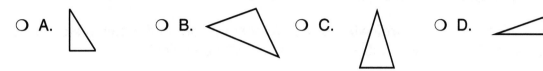

    ○ A.   ○ B.   ○ C.   ○ D.

8. Which of the following figures shows a line of symmetry?

    ○ A.   ○ B.   ○ C.   ○ D.

9. Which of the following pictures does NOT show a polygon?

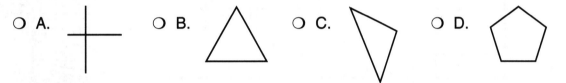

    ○ A.   ○ B.   ○ C.   ○ D.

10. Which of the following shows a picture of an acute, equilateral triangle?

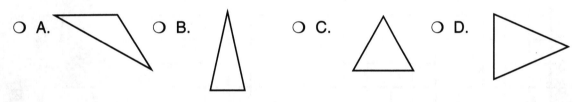

    ○ A.   ○ B.   ○ C.   ○ D.

11. Which of the following shows a scalene triangle?

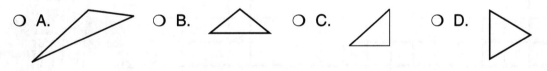

    ○ A.   ○ B.   ○ C.   ○ D.

12. Which of the following shows an equilateral triangle?

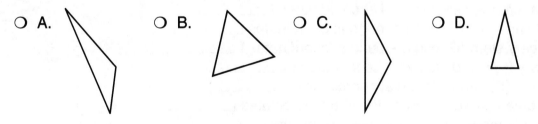

    ○ A.   ○ B.   ○ C.   ○ D.

© Mark Twain Media, Inc., Publishers

Name: _____ Date: _____

Skill: Specifying locations and describing spatial relationships using coordinate geometry and other representational systems

Unit 3: Geometry: *Practice Activity 3*

When finding the location of **coordinate points**, the first number in the pair is the location on the horizontal axis. The second number is the location on the vertical axis.

Example: (5,7) means five units to the right on the horizontal axis and then seven units up on the vertical axis.

Look at the map. Write down the coordinates for each location.

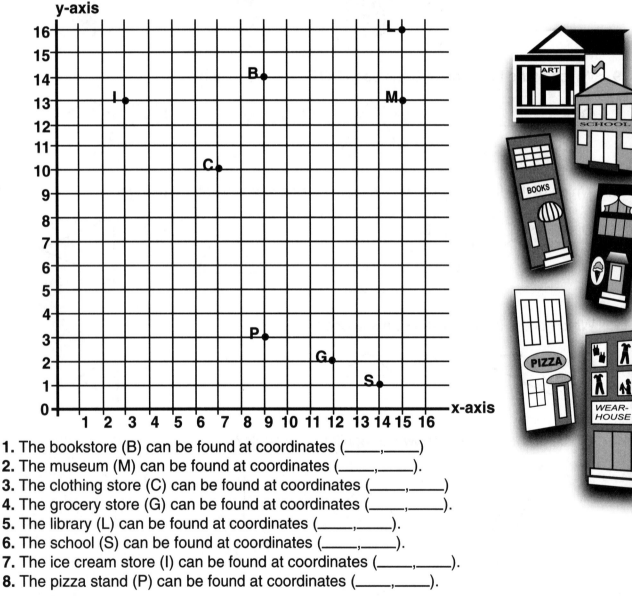

1. The bookstore (B) can be found at coordinates (_____,_____)
2. The museum (M) can be found at coordinates (_____,_____).
3. The clothing store (C) can be found at coordinates (_____,_____)
4. The grocery store (G) can be found at coordinates (_____,_____).
5. The library (L) can be found at coordinates (_____,_____).
6. The school (S) can be found at coordinates (_____,_____).
7. The ice cream store (I) can be found at coordinates (_____,_____).
8. The pizza stand (P) can be found at coordinates (_____,_____).

Extension Activity: Have each student design his/her own city on the map on a piece of grid paper. Give students the following four requirements when creating their cities: (1) each city must have at least eight stores and/or locations; (2) each location must be on a specific coordinate; (3) each city must have a key; and (4) each city must have a name.

Name: _____ Date: _____

Skill: Specifying locations and describing spatial relationships using coordinate geometry and other representational systems

Unit 3: Geometry: *Practice Activity 4*

Follow the directions. Fill in the letters on the graph.

1. Fill in the letter "I" at the coordinates (7,3).
2. Fill in the letter "M" at the coordinates (5,4).
3. Fill in the letter "H" at the coordinates (6,7).
4. Fill in the letter "A" at the coordinates (9,12).
5. Fill in the letter "P" at the coordinates (12,9).
6. Fill in another letter "P" at the coordinates (9,9).
7. Fill in the letter "Y" at the coordinates (5,11).
8. Fill in the letter "N" at the coordinates (8,8).
9. Fill in the letter "O" at the coordinates (11,5).
10. Fill in the letter "W" at the coordinates (12,10).

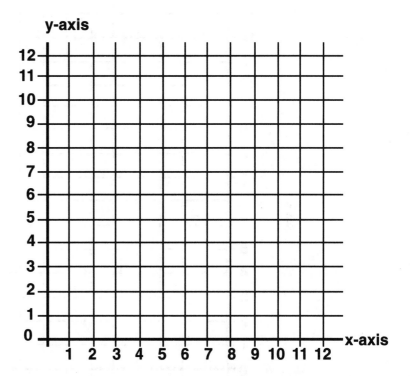

Look at the graph. Find the coordinates of each letter.

11. What are the coordinates of the letter "E"?
    (____,____)
12. What are the coordinates of the letter "N"?
    (____,____)
13. What are the coordinates of the letter "L"?
    (____,____)
14. What are the coordinates of the letter "A"?
    (____,____)
15. What are the coordinates of the letter "R"?
    (____,____)

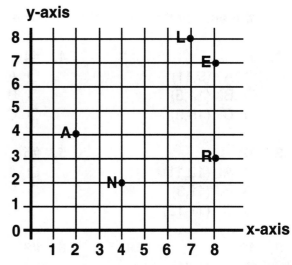

WAKE-UP WORD PROBLEM: Hill Elementary is located 67 miles from Frost Elementary. If Woods Elementary is located an additional 17 miles from Hill Elementary, what is the distance between Frost Elementary and Woods Elementary? _____

Name: _____ Date: _____

Skill: Specifying locations and describing spatial relationships using coordinate geometry and other representational systems

Unit 3: Geometry: *Assessment 2*

Mark the answer that best describes where each number is located on the above grid.

1. #1
   ○ A. (9,11)
   ○ B. (14,5)
   ○ C. (15,9)

2. #2
   ○ A. (12,11)
   ○ B. (11,3)
   ○ C. (11,12)

3. #3
   ○ A. (4,4)
   ○ B. (4,1)
   ○ C. (1,4)

4. #4
   ○ A. (11,12)
   ○ B. (12,10)
   ○ C. (10,12)

5. #5
   ○ A. (11,3)
   ○ B. (3,11)
   ○ C. (10,11)

6. #6
   ○ A. (15,7)
   ○ B. (9,15)
   ○ C. (15,9)

7. #7
   ○ A. (2,6)
   ○ B. (6,4)
   ○ C. (2,4)

8. #8
   ○ A. (11,9)
   ○ B. (9,11)
   ○ C. (9,14)

9. #9
   ○ A. (5,4)
   ○ B. (4,5)
   ○ C. (5,2)

Name: _____ Date: _____

Review of Four Previously Taught NCTM Standards

- **Understanding patterns, relations, and functions**

- **Representing and analyzing mathematical situations and structures using algebraic symbols.**

- **Analyzing characteristics and properties of two- and three-dimensional geometric shapes, and developing mathematical arguments about geometric relationships**

- **Specifying locations and describing spatial relationships using coordinate geometry and other representational systems**

Mark the answer that is represented by the variable.

1. $21 \times y = 189$
    - ○ A. 6
    - ○ B. 9
    - ○ C. 4
    - ○ D. 5

2. $185 \div y = 30$ remainder 5
    - ○ A. 2
    - ○ B. 4
    - ○ C. 6
    - ○ D. 8

Fill in the missing numbers in each pattern.

3. 72, 88, ___, 120, ___, ___
    - ○ A. 114, 138, 152
    - ○ B. 105, 128, 148
    - ○ C. 104, 136, 152
    - ○ D. 104, 136, 151

4. 108, ___, 84, 72, ___, ___
    - ○ A. 96, 58, 52
    - ○ B. 96, 60, 48
    - ○ C. 96, 62, 50
    - ○ D. 96, 61, 48

5. 16, ___, ___, 128, ___, 512
    - ○ A. 24, 48, 192
    - ○ B. 32, 64, 256
    - ○ C. 34, 68, 272
    - ○ D. 42, 84, 336

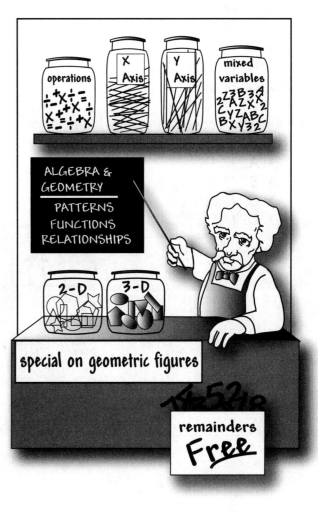

© Mark Twain Media, Inc., Publishers   41

Name: _____ Date: _____

Unit 3: Review of Four Previously Taught NCTM Standards (cont.)

Look at the grid below. Then answer questions 6–9.

6. On which coordinate is the letter "D" located?
   - ○ A. (2,3)
   - ○ B. (3,3)
   - ○ C. (7,1)
   - ○ D. (3,2)

7. On which coordinate is the letter "B" located?
   - ○ A. (3,2)
   - ○ B. (7,1)
   - ○ C. (1,7)
   - ○ D. (5,8)

8. On which coordinate is the letter "C" located?
   - ○ A. (9,10)
   - ○ B. (5,4)
   - ○ C. (10,9)
   - ○ D. (4,5)

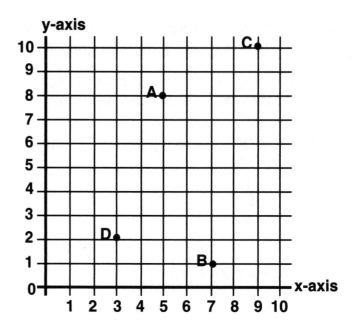

9. On which coordinate is the letter "A" located?
   - ○ A. (7,1)
   - ○ B. (6,2)
   - ○ C. (5,8)
   - ○ D. (4,5)

Name: _____ Date: _____

Skill: Applying transformations and using symmetry to analyze mathematical situations

Unit 3: Geometry: *Practice Activity 5*

Symmetry means that the parts of a figure on either side of a dividing line are identical in size, shape, and position. The two sides are mirror images of each other.

1. Mark the letter of the object that has a line of symmetry.

2. Mark the letter of the object that has a line of symmetry.

3. Mark the letter of the object that has a line of symmetry.

4. Mark the letter of the object that has a line of symmetry.

    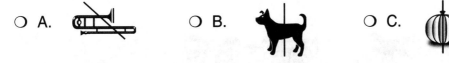

5. Mark the letter of the object that has a line of symmetry.

Read each sentence. Mark true or false.

6. All objects can have only one line of symmetry.
    ○ A. true ○ B. false

7. Symmetry means one side reflects the other.
    ○ A. true ○ B. false

8. All letters have at least one line of symmetry.
    ○ A. true ○ B. false

9. All numbers have at least one line of symmetry.
    ○ A. true ○ B. false

10. Squares, rectangles, and circles do not have lines of symmetry.
    ○ A. true ○ B. false

© Mark Twain Media, Inc., Publishers

Name: _____ Date: _____

Unit 3: Geometry: *Practice Activity 5 (cont.)*

 Just a Tip: A **reflection** can be defined as a flip, which produces a mirror image.

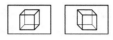

A **rotation** can be defined as a figure that is rotated around a specific point.

A **translation** can be defined as a slide, a figure that is moving along a straight line.

Describe what movement took place between the first and second object.

11. ○ A. reflection
○ B. rotation
○ C. translation

12. ○ A. reflection
○ B. rotation
○ C. translation

13. ○ A. reflection
○ B. rotation
○ C. translation

14. ○ A. reflection
○ B. rotation
○ C. translation

15. ○ A. reflection
○ B. rotation
○ C. translation

WAKE-UP WORD PROBLEM: Ms. McCoy is getting ready for the new school year. She cuts out 717 shapes. Six hundred eighty-eight of the shapes have a line of symmetry. The rest do not. How many of the shapes do not have a line of symmetry?

© Mark Twain Media, Inc., Publishers

Name: _____ Date: _____

Skill: Applying transformations and using symmetry to analyze mathematical situations

Unit 3: Geometry: *Practice Activity 6*

Look at the letter and/or number in each box. Then follow the directions given.

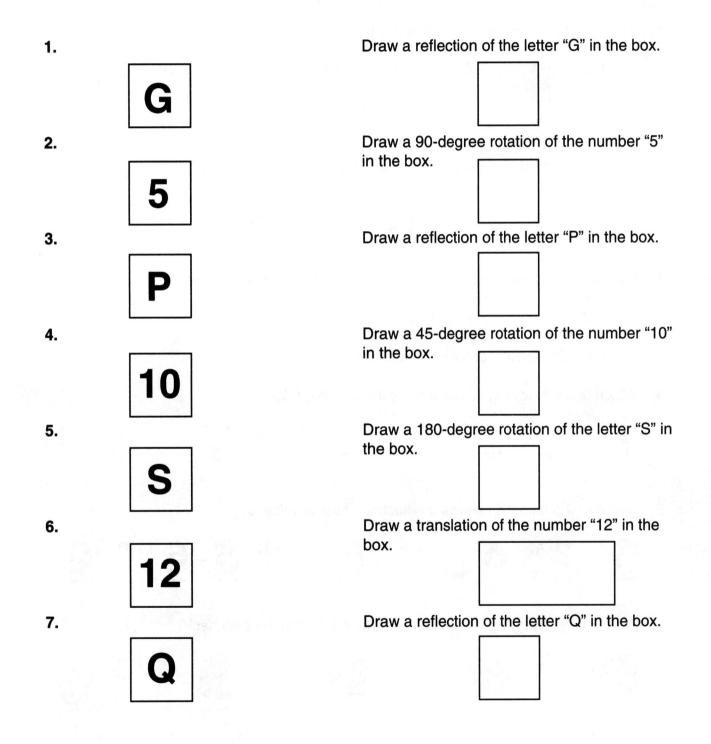

1.

    G

    Draw a reflection of the letter "G" in the box.

2.

    5

    Draw a 90-degree rotation of the number "5" in the box.

3.

    P

    Draw a reflection of the letter "P" in the box.

4.

    10

    Draw a 45-degree rotation of the number "10" in the box.

5.

    S

    Draw a 180-degree rotation of the letter "S" in the box.

6.

    12

    Draw a translation of the number "12" in the box.

7.

    Q

    Draw a reflection of the letter "Q" in the box.

Name: _____ Date: _____

Skill: Applying transformations and using symmetry to analyze mathematical situations

Unit 3: Geometry: *Assessment 3*

Mark the best answer.

1. Which of the following objects has more than one line of symmetry?

   ○ A.   ○ B.   ○ C.   ○ D.

2. Which of the following letters does NOT have a line of symmetry?

   ○ A. A   ○ B. C   ○ C. H   ○ D. F

3. Which of the following statements best describes a line of symmetry?
   ○ A. One side reflects the other.
   ○ B. One side rotates the other.
   ○ C. One side translates the other.
   ○ D. One side overpowers the other.

4. Which of the following shows a translation of the letter "T"?

   T   ○ A. ⊥   ○ B. ⟨   ○ C. T   ○ D. ⊢T

5. Which of the following shows a reflection of the number 6?

   6   ○ A.   ○ B.   ○ C. 6→6   ○ D.

6. Which of the following shows a 90-degree rotation of the backpack?

   ○ A.   ○ B.   ○ C.   ○ D.

Name: _____ Date: _____

Unit 3: Geometry: *Assessment 3 (cont.)*

7. Which of the following shows a translation of the flower in the vase?

○ A. ○ B. ○ C. ○ D.

8. Which of the following shows a 60-degree rotation of the cup of coffee?

○ A. ○ B. ○ C. ○ D.

9. Which of the following has a line of symmetry?

○ A. ○ B. ○ C. ○ D.

10. Which of the following shows a reflection of the wagon?

○ A. ○ B. ○ C. ○ D.

11. Which of the following shows a reflection of the running shoe?

○ A. ○ B. ○ C. ○ D.

Name: _____ Date: _____

Unit 3: Geometry: *Assessment 3 (cont.)*

12. Which of the following shows a 45-degree rotation of the telephone?

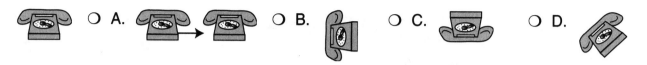

13. Which of the following shows a 180-degree rotation of the golf club?

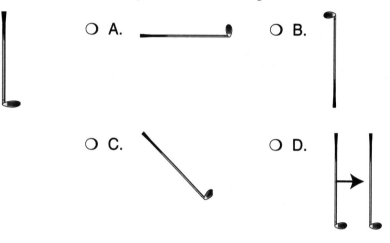

14. Which of the following shows a symmetrical house?

© Mark Twain Media, Inc., Publishers

Name: _____   Date: _____

Skill: Using visualization, spatial reasoning, and geometric modeling to solve problems

Unit 3: Geometry: *Practice Activity 7*

What would a net for each of the following shapes look like? Each net should be able to be folded and copied to create the specified shape. Use your own paper for this activity. Shown below is a sample net for a rectangular prism.

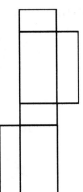

1. Draw a different net from the one shown for a rectangular prism.
2. Draw a net for a cylinder.
3. Draw a net for a cone.
4. Draw a net for a cube.
5. Draw a net for a square pyramid.
6. Draw a net for a triangular pyramid.
7. Draw a net for a triangular prism.

Read the directions provided. Then draw each figure and/or figures in the box.

8. Draw a cylinder in the box.
   Rotate the cylinder 45 degrees.

9. Draw a cube in the box.
   Rotate the cube 90 degrees.

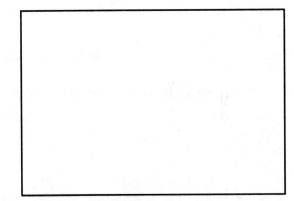

10. Draw a triangle in the box.
    Flip the triangle.

11. Draw a rectangle in the box.
    Show a translation of the rectangle.

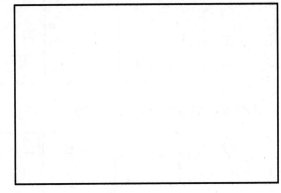

© Mark Twain Media, Inc., Publishers   49

Name: _____ Date: _____

Skill: Using visualization, spatial reasoning, and geometric modeling to solve problems

Unit 3: Geometry: *Practice Activity 8*

Mark the best answer.

1. Which picture shows a vertical reflection of the ice cream cone?

○ A.   ○ B.   ○ C.   ○ D.

2. Which picture shows a rotation of the trapezoid?

○ A.   ○ B.   ○ C.   ○ D.

3. Which picture shows a translation of the book?

○ A.   ○ B.   ○ C.   ○ D.

Read the directions given. Then mark the correct answer. Use your own paper for the drawings.

4. Draw a heart in the corner of the page. Turn the heart 180 degrees. What will it look like?

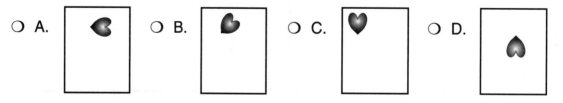

○ A.   ○ B.   ○ C.   ○ D.

5. Draw a cylinder in the middle of the page. Flip the cylinder horizontally. Turn it 90 degrees.

○ A.   ○ B.   ○ C.   ○ D.

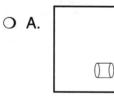  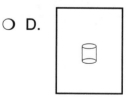

6. Draw a square in the corner of the page. Flip it vertically. Turn it 180 degrees.

○ A.   ○ B.   ○ C.   ○ D.

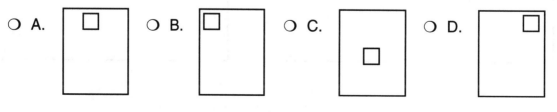

© Mark Twain Media, Inc., Publishers

Name: _____ Date: _____

Unit 3: Geometry: *Practice Activity 8 (cont.)*

7. Mark the choice that correctly shows the result. Draw a triangle. Rotate it twice. Then draw its reflection.

8. Mark the choice that correctly shows the result. Draw a dinosaur. Rotate it once. Then draw its translation.

Just a Tip: A **two-dimensional shape** is a flat shape, a figure on a plane.

☐ **square**

A **three-dimensional shape** can be defined as a space figure.

cube

Read the clues. Select the shape the clues describe.

9. I have four sides. I have two pairs of equal sides.
    ○ A. I am a square.
    ○ B. I am a rectangle.
    ○ C. I am a cube.
    ○ D. I am a rectangular prism.

10. I have six faces. All of my faces are squares.
    ○ A. I am a square.
    ○ B. I am a rectangle.
    ○ C. I am a rectangular prism.
    ○ D. I am a cube.

© Mark Twain Media, Inc., Publishers

Name: _____ Date: _____

Unit 3: Geometry: *Practice Activity 8 (cont.)*

Draw each of the shapes described below in the boxes provided.

11. I have eight sides. All of my sides are equal.

12. Draw a cone in the box provided.

13. Draw a cube in the box provided.

WAKE-UP WORD PROBLEM: Marquee works 40 hours in June. In July, he works an additional 9 hours, and in August, he works 12 more hours than he worked in July. He is paid $7 for each hour that he works. How much money does Marquee earn during June, July, and August?

© Mark Twain Media, Inc., Publishers

Name: _____ Date: _____

Skill: Using visualization, spatial reasoning, and geometric modeling to solve problems

Unit 3: Geometry: *Assessment 4*

Look at figures A and B in each box. Tell whether figure B is a reflection, rotation, or translation of figure A. Mark the correct answer.

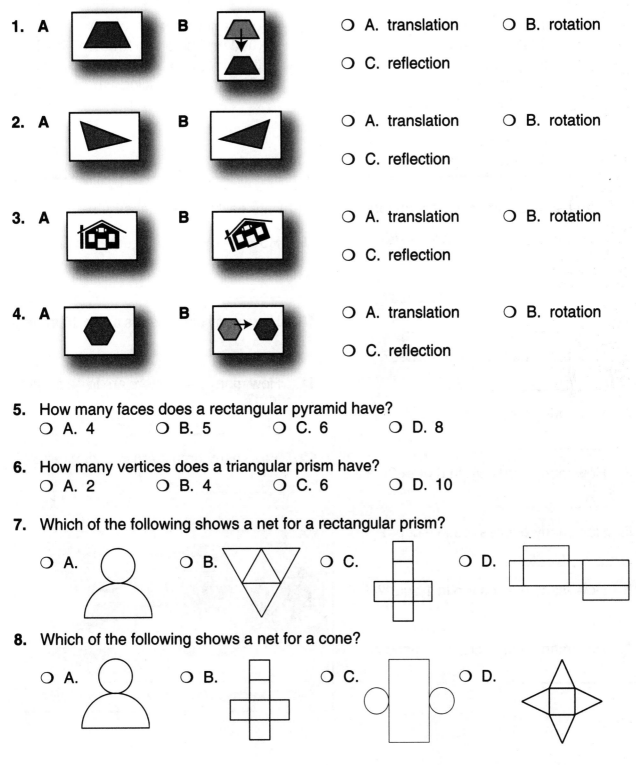

1. A   B   ○ A. translation   ○ B. rotation

           ○ C. reflection

2. A   B   ○ A. translation   ○ B. rotation

           ○ C. reflection

3. A   B   ○ A. translation   ○ B. rotation

           ○ C. reflection

4. A   B   ○ A. translation   ○ B. rotation

           ○ C. reflection

5. How many faces does a rectangular pyramid have?
   ○ A. 4   ○ B. 5   ○ C. 6   ○ D. 8

6. How many vertices does a triangular prism have?
   ○ A. 2   ○ B. 4   ○ C. 6   ○ D. 10

7. Which of the following shows a net for a rectangular prism?

   ○ A.   ○ B.   ○ C.   ○ D.

8. Which of the following shows a net for a cone?

   ○ A.   ○ B.   ○ C.   ○ D.

Name: _____ Date: _____

Skill: Understanding measurable attributes of objects and the units, systems, and processes of measurement

Unit 4: Measurement: *Practice Activity 1*

Customary Measurements	Metric Measurements
1 foot = 12 inches 3 feet = 1 yard 5,280 feet = 1 mile 8 ounces = 1 cup 16 ounces = 1 pound 2 cups = 1 pint 2 pints = 1 quart 4 quarts = 1 gallon	100 centimeters = 1 meter 1,000 millimeters = 1 meter 1,000 meters = 1 kilometer 1,000 grams = 1 kilogram

Translate each customary measurement.

1. How many inches are in 2 yards?

   _____

2. How many feet are in 60 inches?

   _____

3. How many feet are in 48 inches?

   _____

4. How many feet are in 7 miles?

   _____

5. How many yards are in 5 miles?

   _____

6. How many ounces are in 9 cups?

   _____

7. How many ounces are in 1 quart?

   _____

8. How many quarts are in 12 gallons?

   _____

Translate each metric measurement.

9. How many kilometers are in 5,000 meters?

   _____

10. How many centimeters are in 10 meters?

   _____

11. How many millimeters are in 12 centimeters?

   _____

12. How many grams are in 8 kilograms?

   _____

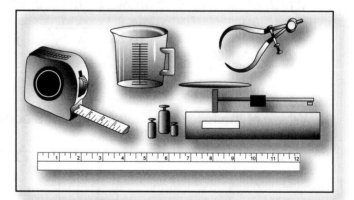

Name: _____ Date: _____

Skill: Understanding measurable attributes of objects and the units, systems, and processes of measurement

Unit 4: Measurement: *Practice Activity 2*

Just a Tip: Area is the number of square units needed to cover a figure or specific space. Find the area by multiplying the length times the width. **L x W = Area**

Example: **The area of a square: 6 inches x 6 inches = 36 square inches.**

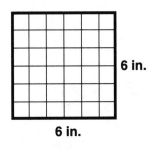

6 in.

Area = 36 square units

Perimeter = 24 units

6 in.

Perimeter is the distance around a closed figure. Find the perimeter by adding the lengths of each side of the figure.

Example: **The perimeter of a square: 6 in. + 6 in. + 6 in. + 6 in. = 24 in.**

Volume is the amount of space occupied by a three-dimensional figure. Find the volume by multiplying the length times the width times the height of a figure. **L x W x H = Volume**

Example: **The volume of a rectangular prism: 8 in. x 7 in. x 3 in. = 168 cubic inches.**

Find the area of each shape.

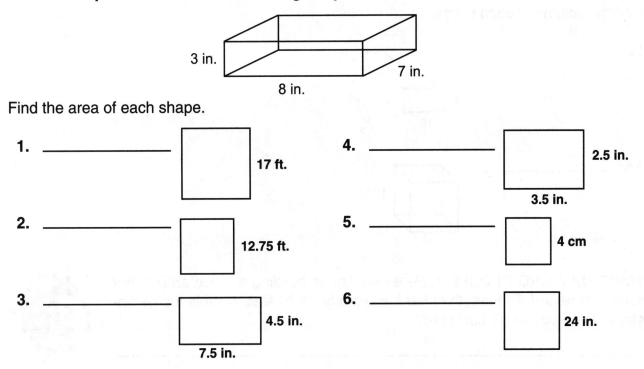

1. _____   17 ft.

2. _____   12.75 ft.

3. _____   4.5 in. 7.5 in.

4. _____   2.5 in. 3.5 in.

5. _____   4 cm

6. _____   24 in.

3 in.   7 in.
8 in.

© Mark Twain Media, Inc., Publishers   55

Name: _____ Date: _____

Unit 4: Measurement: *Practice Activity 2 (cont.)*

Find the perimeter of each shape.

7. _____   □ 21.5 in.

8. _____   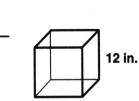 →17 ft.

9. _____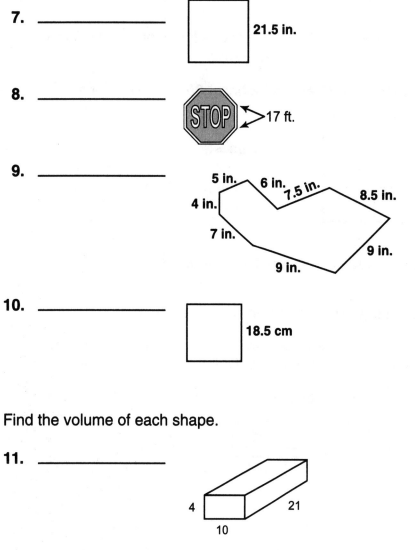

10. _____   □ 18.5 cm

Find the volume of each shape.

11. _____

   4   21
       10

12. _____

   12 in.

WAKE-UP WORD PROBLEM: Penelope Ann is building a fence around her square backyard. The length of her backyard is 25.75 feet. What is the perimeter of Penelope Ann's backyard?

_____

Name: _____ Date: _____

Skill: Understanding measurable attributes of objects and the units, systems, and processes of measurement

Unit 4: Measurement: *Practice Activity 3*

Weight

Circle the best estimate of the unit that should be used to measure each object.

1. a feather
   ounce   pound   ton

2. a microwave oven
   ounce   pound   ton

3. a delivery truck
   ounce   pound   ton

Length

Circle the best estimate of the unit that should be used to measure each object.

4. the distance across a soccer field
   foot   yard   mile

5. the distance between the computer and computer printer
   foot   yard   mile

6. the distance between two cities
   foot   yard   mile

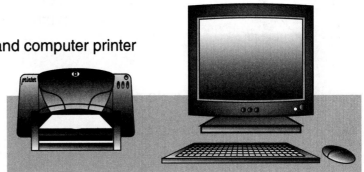

Determine the area of the shape.

7.
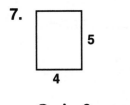
5
4

   ○ A. 9 square units
   ○ B. 20 square units
   ○ C. 12 square units
   ○ D. 22 square units

8.
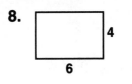
4
6

   ○ A. 24 square units
   ○ B. 20 square units
   ○ C. 22 square units
   ○ D. 10 square units

© Mark Twain Media, Inc., Publishers

Name: _____ Date: _____

Unit 4: Measurement: *Practice Activity 3 (cont.)*

Determine the volume of the shape.

9.

9

○ A. 728 cubic units
○ B. 27 cubic units
○ C. 729 cubic units
○ D. 718 cubic units

10.

4   6
5

○ A. 18 cubic units
○ B. 15 cubic units
○ C. 118 cubic units
○ D. 120 cubic units

Circle the word that best describes the angle.

11.

right   acute   obtuse

12.

right   acute   obtuse

13.

right   acute   obtuse

Fill in the blank for each statement.

14. _____ pounds = 32 ounces

15. 2 feet = _____ inches

16. 5 tons = _____ pounds

17. 5 kilograms = _____ grams

18. 600 centimeters = _____ meters

19. 16 ounces = _____ cups

20. 0.5 pounds = _____ ounces

WAKE-UP WORD PROBLEM: Each side of an octagon measures 19 feet. What is the perimeter of the octagon?

_____

Name: _____ Date: _____

Skill: Understanding measurable attributes of objects and the units, systems, and processes of measurement

Unit 4: Measurement: *Assessment 1*

Mark the choice that is the correct answer.

1. How many quarts are in 6 gallons?
    - ○ A. 24
    - ○ B. 16
    - ○ C. 12
    - ○ D. 20

2. How many ounces are in 10 cups?
    - ○ A. 8
    - ○ B. 18
    - ○ C. 80
    - ○ D. 800

3. How many inches are in 6 feet?
    - ○ A. 18
    - ○ B. 24
    - ○ C. 72
    - ○ D. 64

4. How many inches are in 9 yards?
    - ○ A. 326
    - ○ B. 324
    - ○ C. 108
    - ○ D. 118

5. How many pounds are in 192 ounces?
    - ○ A. 8
    - ○ B. 16
    - ○ C. 18
    - ○ D. 12

6. What is the area of the square?

    - ○ A. 24 square units
    - ○ B. 124 square units
    - ○ C. 144 square units
    - ○ D. 48 square units

    12

7. What is the volume of the cube?

    - ○ A. 324 cubic units
    - ○ B. 314 cubic units
    - ○ C. 5,842 cubic units
    - ○ D. 5,832 cubic units

    18

8. What is the volume of the rectangular prism?

    - ○ A. 108 cubic units
    - ○ B. 180 cubic units
    - ○ C. 116 cubic units
    - ○ D. 18 cubic units

    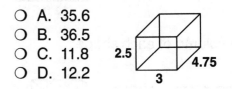
    2   9   6

9. What is the area of the rectangle?

    - ○ A. 183.4 square units
    - ○ B. 206.3 square units
    - ○ C. 178 square units
    - ○ D. 192.1 square units

    11.3
    17

10. What is the volume of the rectangular prism?

    - ○ A. 35.6
    - ○ B. 36.5
    - ○ C. 11.8
    - ○ D. 12.2

    2.5   4.75
    3

Name: _____ Date: _____

Skill: Applying appropriate techniques, tools, and formulas to determine measurements

Unit 4: Measurement: *Practice Activity 4*

Find the perimeter of the irregular shapes.

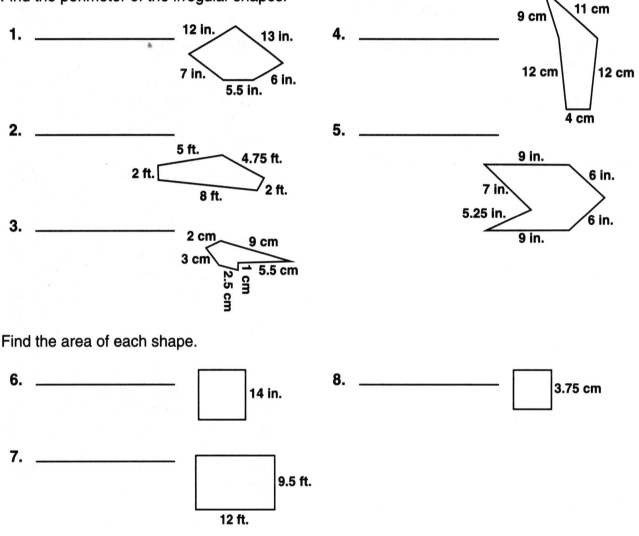

1. _____

2. _____

3. _____

4. _____

5. _____

Find the area of each shape.

6. _____

7. _____

8. _____

Find the volume of each shape.

9. _____

10. _____

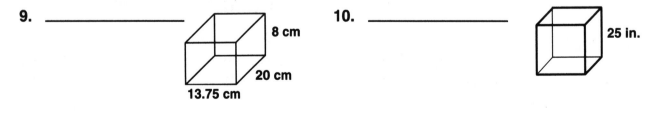

Extension Activity: Draw the following three shapes on your own paper:
1. A shape with a perimeter of 12 inches
2. A shape with an area of 100 cubic units
3. A shape with a volume of 180 centimeters

Name: _____ Date: _____

Skill: Applying appropriate techniques, tools, and formulas to determine measurements

Unit 4: Measurement: *Practice Activity 5*

Mark the choice of the correct answer.

1. Find the perimeter of the shape.
    - ○ A. 21 inches
    - ○ B. 20 inches
    - ○ C. 18 inches
    - ○ D. 16 inches

    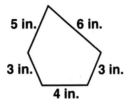

2. Find the area of the shape.
    - ○ A. 14 square units
    - ○ B. 45 square units
    - ○ C. 40 square units
    - ○ D. 25 square units

3. Find the volume of the shape.
    - ○ A. 60 cubic units
    - ○ B. 16 cubic units
    - ○ C. 64 cubic units
    - ○ D. 512 cubic units

4. Find the perimeter of the shape.
    - ○ A. 15 feet
    - ○ B. 30 feet
    - ○ C. 55 feet
    - ○ D. 60 feet

    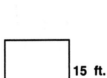

5. Find the perimeter of the shape.
    - ○ A. 22 inches
    - ○ B. 23 inches
    - ○ C. 24.25 inches
    - ○ D. 24.75 inches

6. Find the area of the shape.
    - ○ A. 2 square units
    - ○ B. 1 square unit
    - ○ C. 4 square units
    - ○ D. 7 square units

Name: _____ Date: _____

Unit 4: Measurement: *Practice Activity 5 (cont.)*

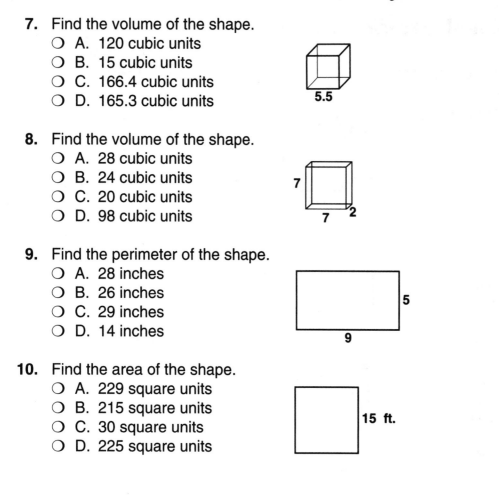

7. Find the volume of the shape.
- ○ A. 120 cubic units
- ○ B. 15 cubic units
- ○ C. 166.4 cubic units
- ○ D. 165.3 cubic units

5.5

8. Find the volume of the shape.
- ○ A. 28 cubic units
- ○ B. 24 cubic units
- ○ C. 20 cubic units
- ○ D. 98 cubic units

7   7   2

9. Find the perimeter of the shape.
- ○ A. 28 inches
- ○ B. 26 inches
- ○ C. 29 inches
- ○ D. 14 inches

5   9

10. Find the area of the shape.
- ○ A. 229 square units
- ○ B. 215 square units
- ○ C. 30 square units
- ○ D. 225 square units

15 ft.

Extension Activity: Record the perimeter of five items around your classroom or bedroom at home.

1. _____

2. _____

3. _____

4. _____

5. _____

Name: _____ Date: _____

Skill: Applying appropriate techniques, tools, and formulas to determine measurements

Unit 4: Measurement: *Assessment 2*

Choose the best answer.

1. Find the volume of the shape.
   - ○ A. 154 cubic units
   - ○ B. 149.6 cubic units
   - ○ C. 154 cubic units
   - ○ D. 148.8 cubic units

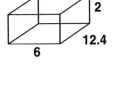

2. Find the area of the shape.
   - ○ A. 625.50 square units
   - ○ B. 625.50 square units
   - ○ C. 650.25 square units
   - ○ D. 600 square units

3. Look at the shape. Mark the number sentence that should be used to find the perimeter of the shape.
   - ○ A. 7.5 + 7.5 + 7.5 + 7.5 + 7.5 =
   - ○ B. 7.5 x 4 =
   - ○ C. 7.5 x 12 =
   - ○ D. 7.5 + 7.5 =

4. Find the perimeter of the shape.
   - ○ A. 57.3
   - ○ B. 53.5
   - ○ C. 53
   - ○ D. 75

5. Find the volume of the shape.
   - ○ A. 2,197 cubic units
   - ○ B. 69 cubic units
   - ○ C. 2,119 cubic units
   - ○ D. 2,009 cubic units

6. Find the area of the shape.
   - ○ A. 24.2 square units
   - ○ B. 94.12 square units
   - ○ C. 93.10 square units
   - ○ D. 93.12 square units

Name: _____ Date: _____

Unit 4: Measurement: *Assessment 2 (cont.)*

7. Look at the shape. Mark the number sentence that should be used to find the perimeter of the shape.
   - ○ A. 13.5 x 8 =
   - ○ B. 13.5 + 13.5 + 13.5 + 13.5 =
   - ○ C. 13.5 x 5 =
   - ○ D. 13.5 ÷ 5 =

13.5 in.

8. Find the perimeter of the shape.
   - ○ A. 41.3 inches
   - ○ B. 47.8 inches
   - ○ C. 48 inches
   - ○ D. 47.2 inches

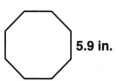

5.9 in.

9. How many pounds in 18 tons?
   - ○ A. 324
   - ○ B. 36
   - ○ C. 3,600
   - ○ D. 36,000

10. How many ounces in 12 cups?
    - ○ A. 96
    - ○ B. 194
    - ○ C. 18
    - ○ D. 144

11. How many centimeters in 4 meters?
    - ○ A. 4,600
    - ○ B. 4,000
    - ○ C. 400
    - ○ D. 40

12. Which is the best unit of measure for the weight of a pillow?
    - ○ A. tons
    - ○ B. ounces
    - ○ C. kilograms
    - ○ D. pounds

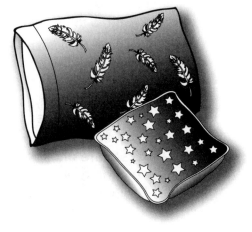

Name: _____ Date: _____

Review of Four Previously Taught NCTM Standards

- **Applying transformations and using symmetry to analyze mathematical situations**

- **Using visualization, spatial reasoning, and geometric modeling to solve problems**

- **Understanding measurable attributes of objects and the units, systems, and processes of measurement**

- **Applying appropriate techniques, tools, and formulas to determine measurements**

Mark the best answer.

1. Which of the following shows a net for a cone?

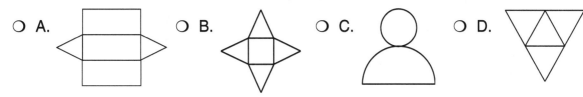

   ○ A.   ○ B.   ○ C.   ○ D.

2. Look at figure A. Mark the answer that best describes the movement between figure A and figure B.
   - ○ A. rotation
   - ○ B. reflection
   - ○ C. translation
   - ○ D. equilateral triangle

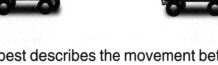

A   B

3. Look at figure A. Mark the answer that best describes the movement between figure A and figure B.
   - ○ A. rotation
   - ○ B. reflection
   - ○ C. translation
   - ○ D. acute triangle

A      B   

4. How many inches are in 21 feet?
   - ○ A. 154
   - ○ B. 254
   - ○ C. 252
   - ○ D. 224

5. How many ounces are in 16 cups?
   - ○ A. 192
   - ○ B. 128
   - ○ C. 196
   - ○ D. 254

© Mark Twain Media, Inc., Publishers

Review of Four Previously Taught NCTM Standards (cont.)

6. What is the area of the rectangle?
   - ○ A. 24 square units
   - ○ B. 30 square units
   - ○ C. 32 square units
   - ○ D. 11.5 square units

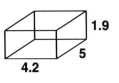

7. What is the volume of the rectangular prism?
   - ○ A. 93.9 cubic units
   - ○ B. 39.9 cubic units
   - ○ C. 39.8 cubic units
   - ○ D. 11.1 cubic units

8. What is the perimeter of the irregular shape?
   - ○ A. 27.8
   - ○ B. 28.9
   - ○ C. 37.8
   - ○ D. 38.5

9. Look at figure A. Mark the answer that best describes the movement between figure A and figure B.
   - ○ A. 90-degree rotation
   - ○ B. 45-degree rotation
   - ○ C. reflection
   - ○ D. translation

10. Which of the following represents an acute triangle?

   ○ A.   ○ B.   ○ C.   ○ D.

11. Which of the following represents a right angle?

   ○ A.   ○ B.   ○ C.

12. Which of the following is the best unit for measuring the distance from one basketball hoop to the other?
   - ○ A. inches
   - ○ B. feet
   - ○ C. yards
   - ○ D. miles

Name: _____ Date: _____

Skill: Formulating questions that can be addressed with data and collecting, organizing, and displaying relevant data to answer them

Unit 5: Data Analysis and Probability: *Practice Activity 1*

Read the graph. Then answer the questions.

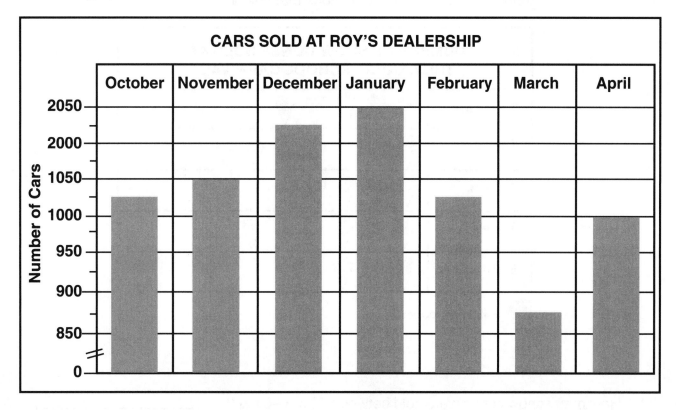

1. How many more cars were sold during January and February than during October and November?

   _____

2. How many fewer cars were purchased during March than during January?

   _____

3. How many total cars were sold during October through January?

   _____

4. How many fewer cars were sold during March and April than during October and November?

   _____

© Mark Twain Media, Inc., Publishers

Name: _____   Date: _____

Skill: Formulating questions that can be addressed with data and collecting, organizing, and displaying relevant data to answer them

Unit 5: Data Analysis and Probability: *Practice Activity 2*

Read the picture graph. Then answer the questions that follow.

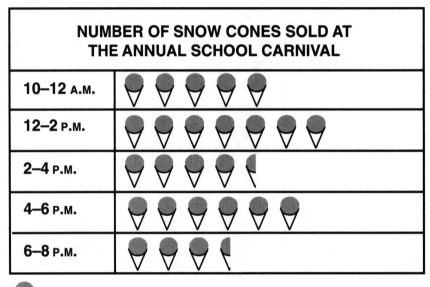

1. How many snow cones were sold between 10 A.M.–8 P.M.? _____

2. Each snow cone costs $0.75. How much money did the snow cone stand make between 4–6 P.M.? _____

3. How many fewer snow cones were sold between 2–4 P.M. than between 12–2 P.M.?

    _____

4. How many total snow cones were sold between 10 A.M.–2 P.M. at the school carnival?

    _____

5. Snow cones go on sale for half price at the end of the carnival. Assuming that twice as many snow cones were sold between 8–10 P.M. as were sold between 6–8 P.M., how many snow cones were sold between 8–10 P.M.?

    _____

Name: _____ Date: _____

Skill: Formulating questions that can be addressed with data and collecting, organizing, and displaying relevant data to answer them

Unit 5: Data Analysis and Probability: *Practice Activity 3*

Read the line graph. Then answer the questions.

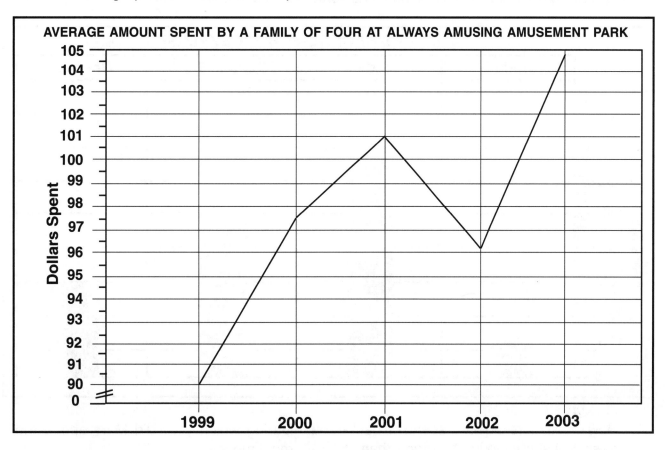

1. On average, how much more money did a family of four spend at Always Amusing Amusement Park during 2003 than during 2000? _____

2. In 2004, on average, a family of four spent $17.75 more visiting Always Amusing Amusement Park than during 2002. How much did a family of four spend visiting Always Amusing Amusement Park during 2004? _____

3. About how much more did it cost a family of four to visit Always Amusing Amusement Park during 2000 than it cost during 1999? _____

4. Assuming that in 1975 it cost half as much for a family of four to visit Always Amusing Amusement Park as it cost in 2000, what was the average cost for a family of four to visit Always Amusing Amusement Park during 1975? _____

5. Based on this graph, which of the following assumptions can be made?
   - ○ A. The cost for an average family of four increased each year.
   - ○ B. The cost for an average family of four generally increased each year.
   - ○ C. The cost for an average family of four generally decreased each year.
   - ○ D. A larger number of people visited during each of the five years.

Name: _____ Date: _____

Skill: Formulating questions that can be addressed with data and collecting, organizing, and displaying relevant data to answer them

Unit 5: Data Analysis and Probability: *Practice Activity 4*

Read the bar graph. Then mark the best answer for each question.

MARY'S BACK-TO-SCHOOL EXPENSES

Grade 3	Grade 4	Grade 5	Grade 6

Dollars Spent — y-axis: 0, 125, 130, 135, 140, 145, 150, 155, 160, 165

Grade 3 ≈ 125; Grade 4 ≈ 154; Grade 5 ≈ 161; Grade 6 ≈ 134

1. How much more did Mary spend on back-to-school shopping in fifth grade than in sixth grade?
   - ○ A. $295
   - ○ B. $25
   - ○ C. $28
   - ○ D. $27

2. During which year did Mary spend the most money?
   - ○ A. grade 6
   - ○ B. grade 4
   - ○ C. grade 3
   - ○ D. grade 5

3. During which year did Mary spend the least amount of money?
   - ○ A. grade 6
   - ○ B. grade 4
   - ○ C. grade 3
   - ○ D. grade 5

4. How much money did Mary spend on back-to-school shopping in third, fourth, and fifth grades combined?
   - ○ A. $441
   - ○ B. $440
   - ○ C. $521
   - ○ D. $618

5. If Mary spends half as much money on back-to-school shopping when she starts seventh grade as she spent when she started sixth grade, how much money will she spend?
   - ○ A. $268   ○ B. $68   ○ C. $67   ○ D. $74

Name: _____ Date: _____

Unit 5: Data Analysis and Probability: *Practice Activity 4 (cont.)*

Read the picture graph. Then mark the best answer.

NUMBER OF DAYS LA'VOTNEY SPENT ON VACATION	
June	☀ ☀ ☀ ☀
July	☀ ☀ ☀ ☀ ☀
August	☀ ☀ ☀ ☀
September	☀

☀ = 4 days spent on vacation

6. How many days did La'Votney spend on vacation during June and July combined?
   ○ A. 36
   ○ B. 34
   ○ C. 4
   ○ D. 28

7. How many more days did La'Votney spend on vacation during August than during September?
   ○ A. 4
   ○ B. 10
   ○ C. 16
   ○ D. 12

8. How many days did La'Votney spend on vacation during June, July, August, and September combined?
   ○ A. 42
   ○ B. 28
   ○ C. 54
   ○ D. 52

9. How many fewer days did La'Votney spend vacationing during August than during June?
   ○ A. 4
   ○ B. 2
   ○ C. 6
   ○ D. 5

10. Which of the following statements is accurate?
   ○ A. La'Votney spent the greatest number of days vacationing during September.
   ○ B. La'Votney spent the fewest number of days vacationing during August.
   ○ C. La'Votney spent the fewest number of days vacationing during September.
   ○ D. La'Votney spent the greatest number of days vacationing during June.

Extension Activity: Have students poll 20 classmates about their favorite flavor of ice cream. Then have students create a picture graph and a bar graph displaying their results.

© Mark Twain Media, Inc., Publishers   71

Name: _____ Date: _____

Skill: Formulating questions that can be addressed with data and collecting, organizing, and displaying relevant data to answer them

Unit 5: Data Analysis and Probability: *Assessment 1*

Read the bar graph. Then mark the correct answers for questions 1–5.

NEW LIBRARY BOOKS AT GREAT HILLS LIBRARY

	September	October	November	December	January	February

Number of Books — axis: 900, 800, 700, 600, 500, 400, 0

1. How many fewer library books were purchased during October than during November?
   - ○ A. 220
   - ○ B. 275
   - ○ C. 250
   - ○ D. 1,325

2. How many fewer books were purchased during December and January than during October and November?
   - ○ A. 175
   - ○ B. 300
   - ○ C. 325
   - ○ D. 375

3. Assuming the library purchased half as many books during March as during January, how many books were purchased during March?
   - ○ A. 1,000
   - ○ B. 300
   - ○ C. 275
   - ○ D. 250

4. How many total books did Great Hills Library purchase during September, October, and November?
   - ○ A. 1,075
   - ○ B. 1,725
   - ○ C. 2,100
   - ○ D. 2,025

5. How many more books were purchased during September and November than during January and February?
   - ○ A. 1,050　　○ B. 400　　○ C. 450　　○ D. 350

Name: _____ Date: _____

Unit 5: Data Analysis and Probability: *Assessment 1 (cont.)*

Read the line graph. Then mark the correct answer for questions 6–10.

AVERAGE MONTHLY TEMPERATURES FOR AUSTIN, TEXAS

6. During which month can you expect Austin, Texas, to have the hottest temperature?
- ○ A. May
- ○ B. June
- ○ C. July
- ○ D. August

7. How much cooler is the average temperature in April than in July?
- ○ A. 17 degrees
- ○ B. 18 degrees
- ○ C. 15 degrees
- ○ D. 12 degrees

8. What is the best estimate of the average temperature in Austin, Texas, during May, June, and July?
- ○ A. 93
- ○ B. 59
- ○ C. 98
- ○ D. 95

9. Which of the following statements is true?
- ○ A. Temperatures are generally warmest in January.
- ○ B. Temperatures are generally coolest in June.
- ○ C. Temperatures are generally coolest in January.
- ○ D. Temperatures are generally warmest in June.

10. What was the difference in temperature between Austin's average temperature during May and August?
- ○ A. 8 degrees   ○ B. 5 degrees   ○ C. 10 degrees   ○ D. 11 degrees

Name: _____ Date: _____

Unit 5: Data Analysis and Probability: *Assessment 1 (cont.)*

Read the picture graph. Then mark the correct answers for questions 11–15.

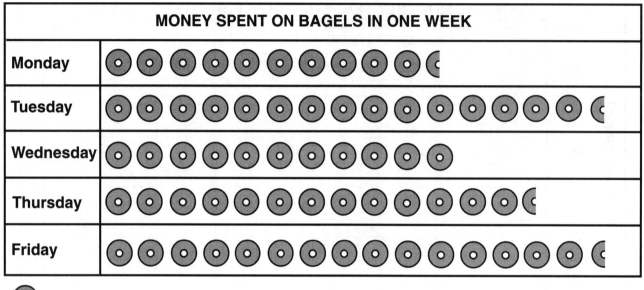

MONEY SPENT ON BAGELS IN ONE WEEK

Monday	⊙⊙⊙⊙⊙⊙⊙⊙⊙⊙(
Tuesday	⊙⊙⊙⊙⊙⊙⊙⊙⊙⊙⊙⊙⊙⊙⊙⊙(
Wednesday	⊙⊙⊙⊙⊙⊙⊙⊙⊙⊙⊙
Thursday	⊙⊙⊙⊙⊙⊙⊙⊙⊙⊙⊙⊙⊙⊙(
Friday	⊙⊙⊙⊙⊙⊙⊙⊙⊙⊙⊙⊙⊙⊙⊙⊙⊙⊙(

⊙ = $1.00

11. Based on the information in the graph, how many bagels could be purchased for $20.00?
    ○ A. 20
    ○ B. 21
    ○ C. 15
    ○ D. 40

12. How much more was spent on bagels on Tuesday and Friday than on Wednesday and Thursday?
    ○ A. $6.75
    ○ B. $6.50
    ○ C. $8.50
    ○ D. $5.25

13. On what day was the least amount of money spent on bagels?
    ○ A. Wednesday
    ○ B. Thursday
    ○ C. Tuesday
    ○ D. Monday

14. What was the total spent for bagels for these five days?
    ○ A. $60.50
    ○ B. $65.00
    ○ C. $66.00
    ○ D. $68.50

15. Based on the information in the graph, which of the following statements is true?
    ○ A. The most money was spent on bagels on Tuesday and Friday.
    ○ B. The least money was spent on bagels on Wednesday.
    ○ C. The most money was spent on bagels on Wednesday and Thursday.
    ○ D. The least money was spent on bagels on Thursday.

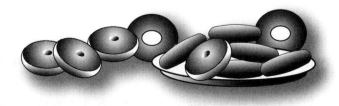

Name: _____ Date: _____

Skill: Selecting and using appropriate statistical methods to analyze data

Unit 5: Data Analysis and Probability: *Practice Activity 5*

Just A Tip: When you are looking for the **median**, you are looking for the middle number in a group of numbers arranged in numerical order. For example, if you are looking for the median of the numbers {3, 6, 4, 3, 1, 7, 9}, first, you have to put the numbers in numerical order {1, 3, 3, 4, 6, 7, 9}. Then, determine the number that is in the middle of all the numbers after they have been put in numerical order. So, the median for the set of numbers given would be 4.

When you are looking for the **mode**, you are looking for the number or numbers that appear most frequently in a set of data. So, if you are looking for the mode for the set of numbers {3, 5, 4, 2, 1, 7, 1, 5, 4, 5}, the mode would be 5, since it appears the most number of times (There are three 5s in the set of data.).

When you are looking for the **range**, you are looking for the difference between the greatest and the least numbers in a group of numbers, so you'll need to subtract. For example, to find the range of the numbers {3, 5, 7, 1, 8, 2, 2, 4}, you would need to find the difference between the largest number (8) and the smallest number (1). Since 8 - 1 = 7, the range of the data is 7.

When you are looking for the **mean**, you are looking for the average. The easiest way to find the average is to add up all the numbers you are averaging and then divide by how many numbers you are averaging. For example, if you are looking for the mean of the numbers {4, 6, 3, 7}, first, add up all four numbers (20). Then, divide 20 by how many numbers you are averaging (4); so, 20 ÷ 4 = 5.

TEAM STANDINGS			
Team	**Wins**	**Losses**	**Ties**
Coyotes	18	2	3
Eagles	15	5	3
Knights	11	5	7
Lions	12	9	2
Rebels	5	13	5

1. What is the mode for this data? _____

2. What is the median number of wins for all of the teams? _____

3. What is the median number of losses for all of the teams? _____

4. What is the median number of ties for all of the teams? _____

5. What is the range for this data? _____

6. Based on this data, how many games can we assume that each team played? _____

© Mark Twain Media, Inc., Publishers

Name: _____   Date: _____

Skill: Selecting and using appropriate statistical methods to analyze data

Unit 5: Data Analysis and Probability: *Practice Activity 6*

AVERAGE NUMBER OF BOOKS CHECKED OUT IN MADISON SCHOOL LIBRARY	
September	‖‖ ‖‖ ‖‖ ‖‖ ‖‖ ‖‖ ///
October	‖‖ ‖‖ ‖‖ ‖‖ ‖‖ ‖‖ ‖‖ ‖‖ ‖‖ /
November	‖‖ ‖‖ ‖‖ ‖‖ ‖‖ ‖‖ ‖‖
December	‖‖ ‖‖ ‖‖ ‖‖ ‖‖ ‖‖ ‖‖ ‖‖ ////
January	‖‖ ‖‖ ‖‖ ‖‖ ‖‖ ‖‖ ‖‖ ////
February	‖‖ ‖‖ ‖‖ ‖‖ ‖‖ ‖‖ ‖‖ ‖‖ //
March	‖‖ ‖‖ ‖‖ ‖‖ ‖‖ ‖‖ ‖‖ ‖‖ ////
April	‖‖ ‖‖ ‖‖ ‖‖ ‖‖ ‖‖ ‖‖ ///
May	‖‖ ‖‖ ‖‖ ‖‖ ‖‖ ‖‖ /

1. What is the range for this data? _____

2. What is the median for this data? _____

3. What is the mode for this data? _____

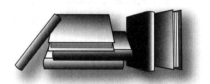

4. The mean number of books checked out between September and May was _____.

NUMBER OF SCHOOL SUPPLIES IN VARIOUS CLASSROOMS						
Room #	Pairs/ Scissors	Bottles/ Glue	Packages/ Crayons	Packages/ Markers	Packages/ Construction Paper	Number/ Protractors
4	15	13	12	16	9	18
6	21	14	17	19	20	13
7	17	14	22	25	18	16
9	11	12	19	24	18	16

5. What is the range for this data? (Do not include room numbers.) _____

6. What is the mode for this data? (Do not include room numbers.) _____

7. What is the median for the # of pairs of scissors for all the classrooms? _____

8. What is the median for the # of crayons for all the classrooms? _____

9. What is the median for the # of packages of markers for all the classrooms? _____

10. What is the median for the # of protractors for all the classrooms? _____

Name: _____ Date: _____

Skill: Selecting and using appropriate statistical methods to analyze data

Unit 5: Data Analysis and Probability: Practice Activity 7

Look at the chart and mark the correct answer for questions 1–2.

LETTERS THAT START FIRST NAMES IN MR. GARCIA'S CLASS							
A	**B**	**C**	**D**	**J**	**K**	**M**	**S**
~~THH~~ /	///	/	/	~~THH~~ //	///	~~THH~~	////

1. Which letter appears the most often in this tally chart?
- ○ A. A
- ○ B. J
- ○ C. M
- ○ D. S

2. The letter that appears most often is called the _____.
- ○ A. range
- ○ B. median
- ○ C. mode
- ○ D. statistic

Look at the chart and mark the correct answers for questions 3–7.

ART CLUB: YEARS STUDENTS WERE BORN				
1985	**1986**	**1987**	**1988**	**1989**
////	~~THH~~ ////	////	~~THH~~	//

3. What is the median for this set of data?
- ○ A. 2
- ○ B. 4
- ○ C. 5
- ○ D. 9

4. What is the mode for this set of data?
- ○ A. 4
- ○ B. 5
- ○ C. 2
- ○ D. 9

5. What is the range for this set of data?
- ○ A. 2
- ○ B. 4
- ○ C. 5
- ○ D. 7

6. In which year were the most children born?
- ○ A. 1985
- ○ B. 1986
- ○ C. 1987
- ○ D. 1989

7. In which year were the fewest number of children born?
- ○ A. 1986   ○ B. 1987   ○ C. 1988   ○ D. 1989

Name: _____ Date: _____

Unit 5: Data Analysis and Probability: *Practice Activity 7 (cont.)*

8. Which statement accurately explains how to find the mode?
    ○ A. Figure out the number that occurs most often.
    ○ B. Determine the middle number in the data set.
    ○ C. Find the difference between the greatest number and the least number.
    ○ D. Name the greatest number.

9. Which statement accurately explains how to find the median?
    ○ A. Figure out the number that occurs most often.
    ○ B. Determine the middle number in the data set.
    ○ C. Find the difference between the greatest number and the least number.
    ○ D. Name the greatest number.

10. Which statement accurately explains how to find the range?
    ○ A. Figure out the number that occurs most often.
    ○ B. Determine the middle number in the data set.
    ○ C. Find the difference between the greatest number and the least number.
    ○ D. Name the greatest number.

11. Look at the following numbers: 4, 3, 7, 9, 2. What is the median of this set of data?
    ○ A. 2
    ○ B. 9
    ○ C. 4
    ○ D. 7

12. Look at the following numbers: 9, 6, 5, 1, 3. What is the median for this set of data?
    ○ A. 1
    ○ B. 5
    ○ C. 6
    ○ D. 3

WAKE-UP WORD PROBLEM: Louise is going to visit her Aunt Mary. She will travel by train and will travel at a rate of 72 miles per hour. Assuming that Louise travels nonstop for seven hours, how many miles will Louise travel to visit her Aunt Mary?

_____

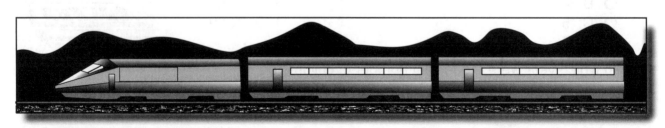

Name: _____ Date: _____

Skill: Selecting and using appropriate statistical methods to analyze data

Unit 5: Data Analysis and Probability: *Assessment 2*

POINTS SCORED BY LIZ	
June	51
July	58
August	69
September	72
October	84
November	73
December	66
January	68
February	72

Use the table above to answer questions 1–5.

1. What is the median of the data?
    - ○ A. 68
    - ○ B. 69
    - ○ C. 72
    - ○ D. 73

2. What is the range of the data?
    - ○ A. 31
    - ○ B. 34
    - ○ C. 33
    - ○ D. 23

3. What is the mode of the data?
    - ○ A. 58
    - ○ B. 73
    - ○ C. 72
    - ○ D. 66

4. About how many points did Liz score, on average, during June and February?
    - ○ A. 60
    - ○ B. 62
    - ○ C. 69
    - ○ D. 68

5. During which month did Liz score the fewest points?
    - ○ A. June
    - ○ B. July
    - ○ C. October
    - ○ D. September

Name: _____ Date: _____

Unit 5: Data Analysis and Probability: *Assessment 2 (cont.)*

Use the tally chart to answer questions 6–10.

NUMBER OF BABIES BORN AT SETON HOSPITAL	
May	卌 卌 卌
June	卌 卌 卌 ///
July	卌 卌 卌 卌 卌 /
August	卌 卌 卌 卌 ////
September	卌 卌 卌 ////
October	卌 卌 卌 卌 卌 /
November	卌 卌 卌 卌 卌 卌 //

6. What is the median of the data?
   - ○ A. 24
   - ○ B. 18
   - ○ C. 26
   - ○ D. 32

7. What is the range of the data?
   - ○ A. 18
   - ○ B. 21
   - ○ C. 18
   - ○ D. 17

8. What is the mode of the data?
   - ○ A. 24
   - ○ B. 15
   - ○ C. 26
   - ○ D. 19

9. On average, how many babies were born each month during May through November?
   - ○ A. 28
   - ○ B. 26
   - ○ C. 23
   - ○ D. 18

10. During which month were the most babies born at Seton Hospital?
    - ○ A. June
    - ○ B. July
    - ○ C. September
    - ○ D. November

11. Find the range of the numbers: 32, 87, 65, 35, 34, 97, 81, 87.
    - ○ A. 87
    - ○ B. 65
    - ○ C. 68
    - ○ D. 72

12. Find the median of the numbers: 288, 311, 209, 304, 335.
    - ○ A. 209
    - ○ B. 288
    - ○ C. 311
    - ○ D. 304

Name: _____   Date: _____

Skill: Understanding and applying basic concepts of probability

Unit 5: Data Analysis and Probability: *Practice Activity 8*

Look at the spinner. Then answer questions 1–3.

1. Tim spins the spinner three times. What color is Tim most likely to land on? _____

2. What color is Tim least likely to land on? _____

3. Why is Tim least likely to land on the color purple? _____

    _____

4. What two colors is Tim equally likely to land on? _____

Jen and Nan are taking turns selecting numbers out of a bag.

5. Which number is Jen least likely to select? _____

6. Which number is Jen most likely to select? _____

7. Which number is Nan least likely to select? _____

8. Which number is Nan most likely to select? _____

Sarah Jane has a bag of colored marbles.

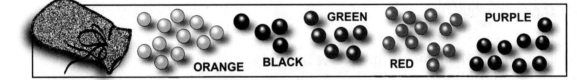

ORANGE   BLACK   GREEN   RED   PURPLE

9. Sarah Jane is most likely to select a _____ marble.

10. Sarah Jane is least likely to select a _____ marble.

Write a fraction to answer question 11.

11. What are Sarah Jane's chances of selecting an orange marble? _____

12. Write one sentence explaining how you came up with a fraction to represent Sarah Jane's chances of selecting an orange marble.

    _____

    _____

Name: _____ Date: _____

Skill: Understanding and applying basic concepts of probability

Unit 5: Data Analysis and Probability: *Practice Activity 9*

Select one of the following words for each of the sentences: **certain**, **impossible**, **most likely**, **least likely**, **equally likely**.

Gerald reaches in the bag several times to pick out a marble.

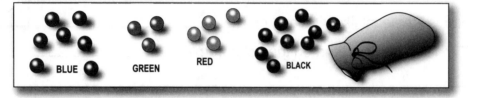

1. It is _____ that Gerald selects a black marble.
   - ○ A. most likely
   - ○ B. least likely
   - ○ C. certain
   - ○ D. impossible

2. It is _____ that Gerald selects a green marble.
   - ○ A. most likely
   - ○ B. least likely
   - ○ C. certain
   - ○ D. impossible

3. It is _____ that Gerald selects an orange marble.
   - ○ A. most likely
   - ○ B. least likely
   - ○ C. equally likely
   - ○ D. impossible

4. Gerald reaches in the bag fifteen times. It is _____ that he selects at least one black marble.
   - ○ A. most likely
   - ○ B. least likely
   - ○ C. equally likely
   - ○ D. certain

Look at the spinner. Then answer questions 5–8.

5. Terrence spins the spinner. It is most likely he will land on _____.
   - ○ A. #1
   - ○ B. #4
   - ○ C. #7
   - ○ D. #9

6. It is least likely he will land on _____.
   - ○ A. #1
   - ○ B. #7
   - ○ C. #4
   - ○ D. #9

Name: _____ Date: _____

Unit 5: Data Analysis and Probability: *Practice Activity 9 (cont.)*

7. It is equally likely that Terrence will land on _____ and _____.
   - ○ A. #9 and #1
   - ○ B. #7 dark and #7 light
   - ○ C. #7 light and #1
   - ○ D. #9 and #4

8. It is impossible that he will land on _____.
   - ○ A. #9
   - ○ B. #8
   - ○ C. #4
   - ○ D. #7

Look at the drawing and answer questions 9–12.

9. Fran reaches in the bag. Which letter is Fran most likely to select?
   - ○ A. R
   - ○ B. M
   - ○ C. P
   - ○ D. S

10. Fran reaches in the bag. Which letter is Fran least likely to select?
   - ○ A. R
   - ○ B. M
   - ○ C. P
   - ○ D. S

11. Fran reaches in the bag ten times. Fran is certain to select at least one _____.
   - ○ A. R
   - ○ B. M
   - ○ C. P
   - ○ D. S

12. Fran reaches into the bag three times. It would be impossible for Fran to select a(n) _____.
   - ○ A. S
   - ○ B. M
   - ○ C. W
   - ○ D. P

WAKE-UP WORD PROBLEM: Movie sales are brisk on the Fourth of July. Two hundred eighty-eight adults and 68 children attend the first matinee of the day of a popular movie. Each adult's ticket costs $5.75, and each child's ticket costs $2.75. How much do all the adults and children pay to watch the first matinee of the day of a popular movie on the Fourth of July?

Name: _____ Date: _____

Skill: Understanding and applying basic concepts of probability

Unit 5: Data Analysis and Probability: *Assessment 3*

Mark the correct answer for each question.

1. Four teams are playing a game. Which answer choice shows the spinner that is fair?

    ○ A. 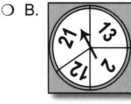   ○ B. 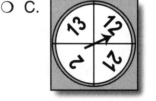   ○ C. 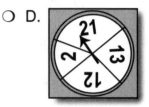   ○ D.

2. Which sentence best explains what makes the spinner above fair?
    ○ A. All numbers have an equal space on the spinner.
    ○ B. The number 21 is the largest number on the spinner.
    ○ C. The number 12 is the smallest number on the spinner.
    ○ D. The numbers each have a designated space on the spinner.

Use the number spinner to answer questions 3–6.

3. Which number is Miriam most likely to spin?
    ○ A. 1
    ○ B. 5
    ○ C. 4
    ○ D. 8

4. Which number is Miriam least likely to spin?
    ○ A. 1
    ○ B. 5
    ○ C. 4
    ○ D. 8

5. Which two numbers is Miriam equally likely to spin?
    ○ A. 5 and 6
    ○ B. 1 and 8
    ○ C. 4 and 5
    ○ D. 4 and 1

6. Which number would be impossible for Miriam to spin?
    ○ A. 1
    ○ B. 7
    ○ C. 8
    ○ D. 5

Name: _____ Date: _____

Unit 5: Data Analysis and Probability: *Assessment 3 (cont.)*

Use the bag of marbles to answer questions 7–10.

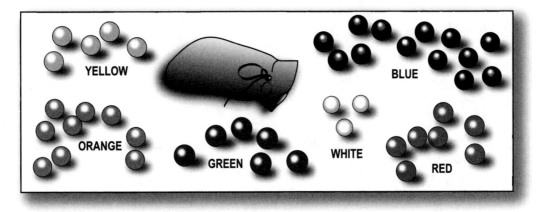

7. Which color is Tonya least likely to select?
   - ○ A. orange
   - ○ B. blue
   - ○ C. green
   - ○ D. white

8. Which color is Tonya most likely to select?
   - ○ A. blue
   - ○ B. red
   - ○ C. green
   - ○ D. yellow

9. Which fraction best represents Tonya's chances of selecting a yellow marble?
   - ○ A. $\frac{7}{45}$
   - ○ B. $\frac{5}{48}$
   - ○ C. $\frac{5}{43}$
   - ○ D. $\frac{21}{19}$

10. Which of the following statements is true?
    - ○ A. There is a 9 out of 54 chance that Tonya will choose orange.
    - ○ B. There is an 8 out of 35 chance that Tonya will choose green.
    - ○ C. There is a 9 out of 43 chance that Tonya will choose orange.
    - ○ D. There is a 10 out of 44 chance that Tonya will choose blue.

Name: _____ Date: _____

End-of-Book Review

Mark the best answer for each problem.

1. $(12 \times 6) \div y = 36$
   - ○ A. 2
   - ○ B. 1
   - ○ C. 4
   - ○ D. 3

2. Find the missing number in the sequence: 119, 112, ____, ____, 91, ____
   - ○ A. 105, 99, 85
   - ○ B. 119, 126, 98
   - ○ C. 105, 98, 84
   - ○ D. 1046, 98, 84

3. How many inches are in 24 feet?
   - ○ A. 188
   - ○ B. 285
   - ○ C. 288
   - ○ D. 218

4. Find the perimeter of the octagon.
   - ○ A. 84 inches
   - ○ B. 106 inches
   - ○ C. 116 inches
   - ○ D. 168 inches

   21 in.

5. Which shape has more than one line of symmetry?

   ○ A.   ○ B.   ○ C.   ○ D.

6. Look at the second and third gingerbread men on the cookie sheet. The gingerbread men are an example of …
   - ○ A. movement
   - ○ B. translation
   - ○ C. reflection
   - ○ D. rotation

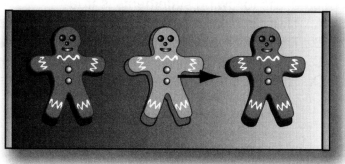

© Mark Twain Media, Inc., Publishers

Name: _____   Date: _____

End-of-Book Review (cont.)

7. 106,873 - 65,902 =
○ A. 41,917
○ B. 40,971
○ C. 172,775
○ D. 40,071

8. Round to the nearest millions place: 6,564,987
○ A. 6,000,000
○ B. 7,000,000
○ C. 7,500,000
○ D. 7,550,000

9. Fill in the missing symbol: 908,878 ____ 980,098
○ A. >
○ B. <
○ C. =
○ D. ÷

10. Which number represents three hundred thirty thousand, six hundred ninety one?
○ A. 330,601
○ B. 3,030,681
○ C. 303,691
○ D. 330,691

11. Find the product: 785 x 211 =
○ A. 165,635
○ B. 1,656,350
○ C. 1,656
○ D. 165,356

12. Find the product: 2,343 x 897 =
○ A. 21,101,671
○ B. 211,671
○ C. 21,101,671
○ D. 2,101,671

13. Look at the bag of numbers. Which number is Hailey most likely to select?
○ A. 101
○ B. 65
○ C. 89
○ D. 87

Name: _____   Date: _____

End-of-Book Review (cont.)

14. Mark the number sentence that should be used to solve the word problem.
Mary and Tim are traveling to Alaska with their grandparents. They will be driving 388 miles every day for ten days. Mary and Tim calculate that their grandparents spend $47.75 each day on gas. How much money do Mary and Tim's grandparents spend traveling to Alaska?
○ A. 318 x 10 =
○ B. 388 x 10 =
○ C. $47.75 x 10 =
○ D. $47.55 x 10 =

15. What is the area of the picture frame?
○ A. 14 square units
○ B. 28 square units
○ C. 168 square units
○ D. 196 square units

14

16. What is the volume of the rectangular prism?
○ A. 480 cubic units
○ B. 25 cubic units
○ C. 96 cubic units
○ D. 560 cubic units

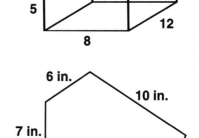

5

12

8

17. Find the perimeter of the irregular shape.
○ A. 40 square inches
○ B. 52 inches
○ C. 40 inches
○ D. 52 square inches

6 in.

10 in.

7 in.

5 in.

12 in.

Use the chart to answer questions 18–20.

LORI'S LEMONADE SALES	
Day	**Glasses Sold**
Monday	6
Tuesday	4
Wednesday	5
Thursday	5
Friday	7

18. What is the mode of the data?
○ A. 4   ○ B. 5   ○ C. 6   ○ D. 7

19. What is the median of the data?
○ A. 4   ○ B. 7   ○ C. 6   ○ D. 5

20. What is the range of the data?
○ A. 1   ○ B. 2   ○ C. 3   ○ D. 4

© Mark Twain Media, Inc., Publishers

Answer Keys

Unit 1: Practice Activity 1 (p. 2–3)

1. 898,432: eight hundred ninety-eight thousand, four hundred thirty-two; 898,432; 800,000 + 90,000 + 8,000 + 400 + 300 + 2
2. 5,001: five thousand one; 5,001; 5,000 + 1
3. 3,212,098: three million, two hundred twelve thousand, ninety-eight; 3,212,098; 3,000,000 + 200,000 + 10,000 + 2,000 + 90 + 8
4. 14,342,009: fourteen million, three hundred forty-two thousand, nine; 14,342,009; 10,000,000 + 4,000,000 + 300,000 + 40,000 + 2,000 + 9
5. 23,098: twenty-three thousand, ninety-eight; 23,098; 20,000 + 3,000 + 90 + 8
6. 789,543; seven hundred eight-nine thousand, five hundred forty-three; 789,543; 700,000 + 80,000 + 9,000 + 500 + 40 + 3
7. 9,001,987; nine million, one thousand, nine hundred eighty-seven; 9,001,987; 9,000,000 + 1,000 + 900 + 80 + 7
8. 12,987; twelve thousand, nine hundred eighty-seven; 12,987; 10,000 + 2,000 + 900 + 80 + 7
9. 21,234,231; twenty-one million, two hundred thirty-four thousand, two hundred thirty-one; 21,234,231; 20,000,000 + 1,000,000 + 200,000 + 30,000 + 4,000 + 200 + 30 + 1
10. 543,323; five hundred forty-three thousand, three hundred twenty-three; 543,323; 500,000 + 40,000 + 3,000 + 300 + 20 + 3
11. 70.08; seventy and eight hundredths; 70.08; 70 + 0.08
12. 6.55; six and fifty-five hundredths; 6.55; 6 + 0.5 + 0.05
13. 0.065; sixty-five thousandths; 0.065; 0.06 + 0.005

Unit 1: Practice Activity 2 (p. 4)

1. 6,000 or 6 thousands
2. 9,000,000 or 9 millions
3. 3 or 3 ones
4. 10,000 or 1 ten thousand
5. 900 or 9 hundreds
6. 30,000 or 3 ten thousands
7. 0.07 or 7 hundredths
8. 2 or 2 ones
9. 1 or 1 one
10. 0.08 or 8 hundredths
11. 6,000 or 6 thousands
12. 30 or 3 tens
13. 0.5 or 5 tenths
14. 0.006 or 6 thousandths
15. 0 or 0 hundred thousands

Unit 1: Practice Activity 3 (p. 5)

The following problems should be circled: #3, #4, #6, and #8

9. 0.4
10. 3.04
11. 5.1
12. 0.17
13. 0.8
14. 6.5
15. 0.25

Unit 1: Practice Activity 4 (p. 6)

1. <
2. <
3. >
4. >
5. <
6. >
7. 45,876; 45,987; 78,876; 78,989
8. 232,123; 235,432; 236,432; 432,342
9. 89,879; 98,008; 98,009; 98,908
10. 234,343; 2,343,212; 2,432,432; 3,432,123
11. 55,434; 54,323; 15,532; 15,232
12. 786,989; 786,878; 786,767; 87,876
13. 144,345; 143,233; 132,343; 123,123
14. 17,876; 7,987; 7,897; 7,809

Unit 1: Assessment 1 (p. 7–8)

1. B
2. B
3. B
4. C
5. B
6. A
7. C
8. A
9. C
10. A
11. D
12. C
13. D
14. C
15. C

Unit 1: Practice Activity 5 (p. 9)

1. 6
2. 192
3. 69
4. 36
5. 26.67
6. 16.67
7. 173.57
8. 32

© Mark Twain Media, Inc., Publishers

9. 156   10. 135.33
11. 3   12. 3,125
13. 37.33   14. 51.43
15. 142.5

WAKE-UP WORD PROB-LEM: Jeremy should deliver approximately 26 packages a day.

Unit 1: Practice Activity 6 (p. 10–11)

1. 26 x 18 = 468; There are 468 students in all.
2. 878 ÷ 3 = 292; She can make 292 bags of cookies.
3. 21 x 24 = 504; He will spend 504 hours at camp.
4. 138 ÷ 67 = 2.029; 2 x67=134; 138 - 134 = 4 on the last page. They will put 2 pictures on each page and 4 pictures on the last page.
5. 3,618 - 911 = 2,707; 2,707 people do not sit in reserved seating.
6. 94 x 9 = 846; She puts 846 cups next to the coffee machine.
7. 175 x 92 = 16,100; He sets up 16,100 chairs.
8. 30 x $6.75 = $202.50; He spends $202.50 on lunch.
9. 876 ÷ 5 = 175.2; They receive about 175 phone calls a day.
10. 102,657 + 16,768 + 12,987 = 132,412; The green truck has 132,412 miles on it.

Unit 1: Practice Activity 7 (p. 12)

1. 6 x 7
2. 6 x 84
3. 5 x 20
4. 9 x 9
5. 15 x 12
6. 432
7. 450
8. 1,560
9. 576
10. 800
11. 2,000
12. 224
13. 1,944
14. 490
15. 900
16. 6 x 3
17. 60 ÷ 5
18. 32 x 2
19. 400 ÷ 4
20. 11 x 10

Wake-Up Word Problem: The lollipops will earn $46 for the store.

Unit 1: Assessment 2 (p. 13–14)

1. C		2. C	
3. D		4. C	
5. A		6. B	
7. C		8. C	
9. D		10. A	
11. B		12. C	
13. B		14. D	
15. C			

Unit 1: Practice Activity 8 (p. 15)

1. 180,000		2. 20,000	
3. 40,000		4. 350,000	
5. 250,000		6. 60,000	
7. 32,000		8. 180,000	
9. 9,000		10. 20,000	
11. 90,000		12. 640,000	

13. 28,000   14. 150,000
15. 4,000   16. 36,000
17. 80,000   18. 36,000
19. 1,000,000 20. 6,300,000

WAKE-UP WORD PROB-LEM: About 4,200 people visit the carnival.

Unit 1: Practice Activity 9 (p. 16)

1. 18,000
2. 24,000
3. 233,000
4. 556,000
5. 11,000
6. 316,000
7. 70,000
8. 240,000
9. 130,000
10. 90,000
11. 90,000
12. 650,000
13. 500,000
14. 2,300,000
15. 900,000
16. 700,000
17. 5,800,000
18. 1,100,000
19. 32,000,000
20. 2,000,000
21. 2,000,000
22. 3,000,000
23. 22,000,000
24. 11,000,000
25. 6,000,000

Unit 1: Practice Activity 10 (p. 17–18)

1. $200 + $100 = $300; Tina spends about $300 at the grocery store.
2. 800 - 200 = 600; 800 + 600 = 1,400; They recycled about 1,400 cans in May and June.

3. $12 \times 6 = 72$; They go swimming about 70 times during a six-month period.
4. $\$4.00 + \$2.00 + \$3.00 = \$9.00 \div 3 = \$3.00$; A milkshake costs about $3.00.
5. $2,000 + 1,000 = 3,000$; About 3,000 campers attend Happy Hills.
6. $20 + 20 + 20 + 30 + 30 + 40 = 160 \div 6 = 26.7$; They go out to eat about 27 times each month.
7. $500 - 300 = 200$; Her sister has about 200 more stickers.
8. $1,000 + 2,000 + 2,000 = 5,000$; About 5,000 students are enrolled in the three elementary schools.
9. $\$6.00 + \$6.00 + \$9.00 + \$4.00 = \$25.00$; They spend about $25 for dinner.

Unit 1: Assessment 3 (p. 19–20)

1.	C	2.	B
3.	B	4.	D
5.	B	6.	B
7.	B	8.	C
9.	D	10.	A
11.	D	12.	C
13.	A	14.	D
15.	A	16.	C
17.	D	18.	C
19.	B	20.	C

Unit 1: Review (p. 21–22)

1.	D	2.	B
3.	A	4.	C
5.	B	6.	D
7.	C	8.	B

9.	C	10.	D
11.	D	12.	C
13.	B	14.	A
15.	C		

Unit 2: Practice Activity 1 (p. 23)

1. 107, 71, 59
2. 128, 2,048, 8,192
3. 81, 100, 176
4. 212, 203
5. 144, 1,152
6. 45, 63, 99
7. 58, 106, 122
8. 66, 93, 174
9. G, M, P
10. R, Q
11. M, N, P
12. #13, 6:44 A.M., 9:46 A.M.
#19, 9:55 A.M., 12:57 P.M.
#25, 2:01 P.M., 5:03 P.M.
#31, 5:15 P.M., 8:17 P.M.
#37, 9:03 P.M., 12:05 A.M.

Unit 2: Practice Activity 2 (p. 24–25)

1.	B	2.	C
3.	A	4.	A
5.	C	6.	B
7.	B	8.	A
9.	B	10.	C
11.	B	12.	A
13.	C	14.	B
15.	C		

Unit 2: Assessment 1 (p. 26–27)

1.	B	2.	D
3.	A	4.	B
5.	B	6.	C
7.	A	8.	A
9.	D		

Unit 2: Practice Activity 3 (p. 28)

1.	15	2.	6
3.	7	4.	3
5.	143	6.	3,546
7.	5	8.	10
9.	16	10.	7,486
11.	878	12.	6
13.	<	14.	>
15.	<	16.	<
17.	=	18.	>
19.	>	20.	=

Wake-Up Word Problem: He had $43.02 before he bought presents.

Unit 2: Practice Activity 4 (p. 29)

1.	B	2.	A
3.	C	4.	C
5.	C	6.	A
7.	B	8.	A
9.	B	10.	B
11.	A	12.	C
13.	A	14.	B
15.	B		

Unit 2: Assessment 2 (p. 30)

1.	A	2.	A
3.	A	4.	B
5.	A	6.	B
7.	B	8.	C
9.	C	10.	A
11.	A	12.	B
13.	C	14.	A
15.	A		

Unit 3: Practice Activity 1 (p. 31–32)

1. triangular prism
2. hexagon
3. cylinder
4. cone
5. pyramid
6. sphere

© Mark Twain Media, Inc., Publishers

7. rectangular prism
8. cube
9. obtuse
10. acute
11. acute
12. right
13. Students should have circled the two congruent hexagons.
14. Students should have circled the two congruent A's.
15. Students should have circled the two congruent umbrellas.
16. Not a polygon
17. Polygon
18. Not a polygon

Unit 3: Practice Activity 2 (p. 33–35)
1. equilateral
2. acute
3. scalene
4. obtuse
5. isosceles
6. sphere
7. cylinder
8. rectangular prism
9. B
10. C
11. A
12. O
13. M
14. scalene
15. equilateral
16. equilateral
17. isosceles
18. scalene

Wake-Up Word Problem:
She collects 17,232 pencils.

Unit 3: Assessment 1 (p. 36–37)
1. D   2. C

3. C   4. A
5. C   6. A
7. A   8. D
9. A   10. C
11. A   12. B

Unit 3: Practice Activity 3 (p. 38)
1. (9,14)   2. (15,13)
3. (7,10)   4. (12,2)
5. (15,16)   6. (14,1)
7. (3,13)   8. (9,3)

Unit 3: Practice Activity 4 (p. 39)
1–10.

11. (8,7)
12. (4,2)
13. (7,8)
14. (2,4)
15. (8,3)

Wake-Up Word Problem:
The distance is 84 miles.

Unit 3: Assessment 2 (p. 40)
1. B   2. A
3. C   4. B
5. A   6. C
7. A   8. B
9. A

Unit 3: Review (p. 41–42)
1. B   2. C
3. C   4. B

5. B   6. D
7. B   8. A
9. C

Unit 3: Practice Activity 5 (p. 43–44)
1. A   2. A
3. C   4. B
5. C   6. B
7. A   8. B
9. B   10. B
11. A   12. B
13. A   14. C
15. A

Wake-Up Word Problem:
Twenty-nine of the shapes do not have a line of symmetry.

Unit 3: Practice Activity 6 (p. 45)
Students should have drawn the following:
1. a reflection of "G"
2. a 90° rotation of "5"
3. a reflection of "P"
4. a 45° rotation of "10"
5. a 180° rotation of "S"
6. a translation of "12"
7. a reflection of "Q"

Unit 3: Assessment 3 (p. 46–48)
1. A   2. D
3. A   4. D
5. B   6. B
7. A   8. A
9. D   10. C
11. C   12. D
13. B   14. D

Unit 3: Practice Activity 7 (p. 49)
Students should have drawn nets for the following:
1. rectangular prism
2. cylinder

© Mark Twain Media, Inc., Publishers

3. cone
4. cube
5. square pyramid
6. triangular pyramid
7. triangular prism
8. cylinder rotated 45°
9. cube rotated 90 degrees
10. triangle flipped
11. translation of rectangle

Unit 3: Practice Activity 8 (p. 50–52)

1. D   2. A or B
3. C   4. D
5. A   6. B
7. D   8. A
9. A or B   10. D
11. Students should have drawn an octagon.
12. Students should have drawn a picture of a cone.
13. Students should have drawn a picture of a cube.

Wake-Up Word Problem: He earns $1,050.00 in June, July, and August.

Unit 3: Assessment 4 (p. 53)

1. A   2. C
3. B   4. A
5. B   6. C
7. D   8. A

Unit 4: Practice Activity 1 (p. 54)

1. 72   2. 5
3. 4   4. 36,960
5. 8,800   6. 72
7. 32   8. 48
9. 5   10. 1,000
11. 120   12. 8,000

Unit 4: Practice Activity 2 (p. 55–56)

1. 289 square feet
2. 162.5625 square feet
3. 33.75 square inches
4. 8.75 square inches
5. 16 square centimeters
6. 576 square inches
7. 86 inches
8. 136 feet
9. 56 inches
10. 74 centimeters
11. 840 cubic units
12. 1,728 cubic inches

Wake-Up Word Problem: The perimeter of her backyard is 103 feet.

Unit 4: Practice Activity 3 (p. 57–58)

1. ounce   2. pound
3. ton   4. yard
5. feet   6. mile
7. B   8. A
9. C   10. D
11. right   12. obtuse
13. acute   14. 2
15. 24   16. 10,000
17. 5,000   18. 6
19. 2   20. 8

Wake-Up Word Problem: The perimeter of the octagon is 152 feet.

Unit 4: Assessment 1 (p. 59)

1. A   2. C
3. C   4. B
5. D   6. C
7. D   8. A
9. D   10. A

Unit 4: Practice Activity 4 (p. 60)

1. 43.5 inches
2. 21.75 feet

3. 23 centimeters
4. 48 centimeters
5. 42.25 inches
6. 196 square inches
7. 114 square feet
8. 14.06 square centimeters
9. 2,200 cubic centimeters
10. 15,625 cubic inches
Extension: Teacher check.

Unit 4: Practice Activity 5 (p. 61–62)

1. A   2. B
3. D   4. D
5. C   6. B
7. C   8. D
9. A   10. D

Unit 4: Assessment 2 (p. 63–64)

1. D   2. C
3. B   4. C
5. A   6. D
7. C   8. D
9. D   10. A
11. C   12. B

Unit 4: Review (p. 65–66)

1. C   2. C
3. B   4. C
5. B   6. B
7. B   8. D
9. B   10. D
11. B   12. B or C

Unit 5: Practice Activity 1 (p. 67)

1. 1,000
2. 1,175
3. 6,150
4. 200

© Mark Twain Media, Inc., Publishers

Unit 5: Practice Activity 2
(p. 68)
1. 1,248
2. $216.00
3. 120
4. 576
5. 336

Unit 5: Practice Activity 3
(p. 69)
1. $7.25
2. $114.00
3. $7.50
4. $48.75
5. B

Unit 5: Practice Activity 4
(p. 70–71)
1. D　　　2. D
3. C　　　4. A
5. C　　　6. B
7. B　　　8. D
9. B　　　10. C

Unit 5: Assessment 1
(p. 72–74)
1. B　　　2. D
3. C　　　4. C
5. B　　　6. D
7. C　　　8. A
9. C　　　10. C
11. A　　　12. B
13. D　　　14. C
15. A

Unit 5: Practice Activity 5
(p. 75)
1. 5　　　2. 12
3. 5　　　4. 3
5. 16　　　6. 23

Unit 5: Practice Activity 6
(p. 76)
1. 15　　　2. 39
3. 44　　　4. 39

5. 16　　　6. 16 & 18
7. 15 & 17　8. 17 & 19
9. 19 & 24　10. 16

Unit 5: Practice Activity 7
(p. 77–78)
1. B　　　2. C
3. B　　　4. A
5. D　　　6. B
7. D　　　8. A
9. B　　　10. C
11. C　　　12. B

Wake-Up Word Problem:
Louise will travel 504 miles.

Unit 5: Assessment 2
(p. 79–80)
1. B　　　2. C
3. C　　　4. B
5. A　　　6. A
7. D　　　8. C
9. C　　　10. D
11. B　　　12. D

Unit 5: Practice Activity 8
(p. 81)
1. green
2. purple
3. It has the smallest space.
4. orange and yellow
5. 8
6. 13
7. 8
8. 13
9. red
10. black
11. $\frac{11}{42}$
12. The top number is the number of orange marbles, and the bottom number represents the total number of marbles in the bag.

Unit 5: Practice Activity 9
(p. 82–83)
1. A　　　2. B
3. D　　　4. D
5. C　　　6. A
7. B　　　8. B
9. B　　　10. C
11. B　　　12. C

Wake-Up Word Problem: In all, they spent $1,843.00 to watch the popular movie.

Unit 5: Assessment 3
(p. 84–85)
1. C　　　2. A
3. C　　　4. A
5. A　　　6. B
7. D　　　8. A
9. C　　　10. C

End-of-Book Review
(p. 86–87)
1. A　　　2. C
3. C　　　4. D
5. D　　　6. B
7. B　　　8. B
9. B　　　10. D
11. A　　　12. D
13. B　　　14. C
15. D　　　16. A
17. C　　　18. B
19. D　　　20. C